Called
to Be
HOLY

Called

to Be

HOLY

Linda Brumley

Called to Be Holy
© 2021 by Linda Brumley. ISBN: 978-1-953623-02-7.

Printed in the United States of America.

Unless otherwise indicated, all Scripture references are from the Holy Bible, New International Version, copyright 1973, 1978, 1984, 2011 by the International Bible Society. Used by permission of Zondervan Bible Publishers.

Cover design by Roy Appalsamy of Toronto, Canada. The text faces are set in Karmina, Agilo Handwriting and Agenda.

Copy Editor: Amy Morgan. Interior layout by Toney Mulhollan.

Illumination Publishers is committed to caring wisely for God's creation and uses recycled paper whenever possible.

About the author: Linda Brumley has served in the ministry in San Diego, Chicago, Denver and Seattle. She now lives in San Diego, California. Her greatest joy in life is friends and family (four children and ten grandchildren). Because she feels so blessed to have learned from mentors in her life, she hopes to offer that same blessing to women that God enables her to influence for him. Linda's  other books include *My Beggar's Purse* and *Finding Your Path to Forgiveness* and a contributor to *Golden Rule Membership* by Dr. John M. Oakes.

www.ipibooks.com
6010 Pinecreek Ridge Court
Spring, Texas 77379-2513

Contents

Acknowledgements

Thank you to Toney Mulhollan at Illumination Publishers for believing that I have something worthwhile to share in print.

I was thrilled to learn that Amy Morgan would be my editor for this book. Her keen eye and deep faith are a great blessing.

Thank you to my daughter Meredith, who just happened to be in town when my computer and I were not communicating well. Meredith came with her unusual skill and saved the day (and my manuscript)!

I'm so grateful for the valuable input of the friends who graciously read my first draft and gave me their impressions and insights—Mary, Alice, Lisa, Loidy, and Kerry—especially Kerry! Her valuable suggestions made me think I should claim her as a coauthor.

Most of all, thank you to God for revealing his holy nature in writing in the Bible. And thank you to God for giving me Ron Brumley to walk beside me on this life journey.

Dedication

To Gretchen, my daughter, my counselor, my friend,
who shines with every fruit of God's Spirit.

Introduction

I'm a doer. It's hard for me to be still. I'm not a great connector, although I thought I was. I thought the people I was doing it all for felt connected to me. Eventually, I learned that my motivation in part was not a great love for the people I served, but simply that I get my self-worth from feelings of accomplishment. I knew how to do some holy stuff, but I fell short of being wholly holy. I have noticed the same sad tendency in a few others. It is far easier to assess success from checking off items on a to-do list than to stay in tune with our heart motivations.

Satan will pull us in one direction or another: too still or too busy. I am not writing this only to help my fellow doers. It is also for the be-ers, the ones who are, perhaps, too still. It takes both the doing and the being to be holy. We will never reach the perfect balance—only Jesus did that—but a healthy self-awareness and an effort to overcome some natural tendencies can move those seeking holiness closer to that wonderful goal of Christlikeness.

Upon hearing the word "holy," what pops into your mind? Holy Bible? Holy God? Do you mentally search for a synonym—sacred, pure, sinless, perfect, pious, or religious—thinking one of those exposes its depths of meaning?

In both the original Hebrew and Greek, the word "holy" is most often defined as simply "set apart." God claimed this distinction for himself early on: "I am the Lord your God... I am holy" (Leviticus 11:44–45).

God went to a lot of trouble to clarify his singular character for the Jews, because they had been in captivity in Egypt for 400-plus years when by inspiration Moses penned Leviticus. The Egyptians had multiple idols that they considered to be gods. If it moved, they worshipped it. Living inundated by those images for more than four centuries was confusing for the Jews. They still believed in Jehovah, but they thought they just had the *best* god, not the only God. Still, they wondered why he had left them in such miserable conditions for so long.

With idolatry so rampant, God had to be sure they understood that he was set apart. With the ten plagues, Jehovah differentiated himself and demonstrated his superiority over every Egyptian idol: "I will bring judgment on all the gods of Egypt. I am the Lord" (Exodus 12:12).

God set himself apart by demonstrating his superior power. Pow, Nile River! (Exodus 7:17). Pow, sun, moon and stars! (Exodus 10:21). Pow, Pharaoh! (Exodus 11:5). Jehovah proved himself to be the most powerful, but it was centuries more before the Jews finally acknowledged him as the only God and, at last, never returned to idolatry again. Until then, they had not set him apart in their hearts.

In Western culture we don't have much idolatry in the classic sense. Few of us have graven images in our homes. Even a stone Buddha is more often exotic décor instead of an icon. Nevertheless, there are many things that compete for our devotion. It is easy to lose sight of the things that matter most. Even when we believe in God and claim Jesus as Lord, we may misinterpret and undervalue the call to be holy. We may rely on doctrinal accuracy, superficial worship, robotic prayer lists, and the busyness of good deeds while neglecting our inner selves and our soul-connection with God.

God alone is completely holy. He is set apart in every facet of his being. He calls us, his people, to be holy (II Peter 3:11–12). We can only learn to partake of his holiness by knowing what he is like so we can imitate him and access whatever part of his holiness we are able to grasp. This should be a focus of every Christian because "without holiness no one will see the Lord" (Hebrews 12:14).

I have been thinking about the outline for this book for several years because I have come to have an increasing concern about unholiness, both within myself and within the fellowship with which I worship. I hear little expressed about the sins of the heart. Public lessons often center on the need to be busy serving God or, conversely, the need to feel secure in our salvation. Certainly, both of these topics are crucial, but I don't hear much about making every effort to pursue the fruits of the Spirit, nor do I hear many confessions of weakness in this area. A couple of times when I have confessed impatience or a lack of love or a harsh reply, I have been sort of patted on the head as if it didn't matter. We've got to be different, set apart. How else will the world recognize a different Spirit within us? We must be about the work of becoming holy. We must talk about it, study it, and help each other with it.

This has been a scary book to write. With every chapter I have seen my own failings and how much I need to grow in holiness. I offer these thoughts to you with deep humility. I surely don't want to be negative or diminish the all-sufficient grace of God, but neither do I want to downplay God's desire that we imitate his holiness.

I hope this book will be a benefit to you as you pursue the nature of God in answering his plea to you to be holy. I have certainly been blessed by writing it.

For by one sacrifice he has made perfect forever those who are being made holy. (Hebrews 10:14)

God bless you!

The Bible gives me a deep, comforting sense that "things seen are temporary, and things unseen are eternal." –Helen Keller

Chapter 1

The Holy Unseen

Helen Keller understood from the perspective of physical blindness what Paul meant in II Corinthians 4:18: "So we fix our eyes not on what is seen, but on what is unseen, since what is seen is temporary, but what is unseen is eternal." Believing in the promises and truths of the Bible takes faith. Being blind offered Keller a vision of truth that sighted people may miss. Because we can see, we tend to be distracted—even dazzled—by the chaotic yet appealing world around us. It requires deliberate focus on unseen things to appreciate their value.

Our eyes can deceive us. They can make us desire frivolous things and even think we need them. The busyness of life can consume us and make us replace important demands with the temporally urgent. We become inattentive to unseen consequences. All eternal things—God, heaven, hell, Satan—must be accepted by faith. There is plenty of visible evidence, but even that takes a special kind of lens and some deductive reasoning (Romans 1:20). The lens must be cleared of preconceived notions and prejudice. We must be openhearted and unbiased.

Jesus said, "God is spirit" (John 4:24). What does spirit look like? It is not characterized by or constrained by physical features. Yet God says he wants us to resemble him by imitating him. "Be imitators of God, as beloved children" (Ephesians 5:1 ESV). This is one of my favorite scriptures. I love knowing that God wants me to look like him. What an honor! And what a high calling. I can't have his nose or the color of his eyes, because he is spirit. He wants me to look like the essence of his being, his character, his nature. I need to know what his spirit looks like in order to imitate it—I need to see the unseen.

On one occasion Jesus leveled a scorching judgment aimed at "the Jews who had believed him" (John 8:31–44): "You belong to your father, the devil, and you want to carry out your father's desires." It is clear here that just believing will not gain God's approval. I doubt anyone in that audience thought the desire of their hearts was to assist the devil, but that's how Jesus saw it. His hearers had their eyes closed to the kind of introspection and commitment to growth that could have saved them.

While introspection is revealing and needed, it can only take us so far. An inward focus can be paralyzing. But "fixing our eyes on Jesus" and coming to know the nature of God will clarify our aim and energize our efforts.

> The essence of true holiness consists in conformity to
> the nature and will of God.   –Samuel Lucas

Character and nature, the hidden inner man, the reasoning, the attitudes, the prejudices, the moods, and the motivations— these can be assumed, but not verified, by behavior. Here is what I mean: I may do something that appears incredibly loving, but I may be motivated by looking good (pride). I may do something that appears sacrificial, like making a big charitable donation, but I may have been motivated by a tax break (selfishness). Only God knows. I may even fool myself.

Growing to look like God, who is spirit, is more complex than simply changing behavior, although that is a good and necessary beginning. But God, who searches the heart, is looking for more. And we should be looking for more from ourselves. God simply will not buy impure motives. David, a man after God's own heart (Acts 13:22), understood this when he instructed his son in I Chronicles 28:9:

> *"And you, my son Solomon, acknowledge the God of your father, and serve him with wholehearted devotion and with a willing mind, for the LORD searches every heart and understands every desire and every thought. If you seek him, he will be found by you; but if you forsake him, he will reject you forever."*

Holiness, beyond just being set apart, belongs in the sphere of the sacred. The Tesla has features that set it apart from other automobiles, but it is not holy. From beginning to end, the Bible reveals the holiness of God and announces his call to his followers to be holy. His desire for our holiness has been misunderstood and applied to externals. Sincere people have dictated manners of dress, observance of certain traditions, levels of isolation, or even self-righteous behavior in the name of holiness. (Of course, the birthplace of self-righteousness is in the attitudes of the heart, and God sees those.) Conversely, the fear of *appearing* self-righteous has caused some to avoid being set apart from the world. But face it, holiness is what we are called to by God.

> *"Be holy because, I the LORD your God, am holy." (Leviticus 19:2)*

> *For he chose us in him before the creation of the world to be holy and blameless in his sight. (Ephesians 1:4)*

But just as he who called you is holy, so be holy in all you do. (I Peter 1:15)

"Be like me!" That is God's appeal to us. There is no higher calling, and no greater honor than to be chosen by God to be holy. But is God asking us to be perfect? God is perfect; does holy equal perfect? Perfection is the minimum requirement for admission into heaven, so it matters supremely. While we are on that path of increasing holiness, we have a great comforting assurance found in I Corinthians 1:30: "You are in Christ Jesus, who has become for us... our righteousness, holiness, and redemption." What a gift! What we could not achieve, Jesus achieved and gave to us. But make no mistake: there is a partnership involved. We must cooperate with God to become as holy as we can.

For by one sacrifice, he has made perfect forever those who are being made holy. (Hebrews 10:14)

The gift of perfection is not one to be taken for granted. It is offered only to those who are in the process of being made holy. How does God make us holy? It is through our imitation of the One who is holy.

Holiness is sometimes evident on the surface, but in a damning discourse, recorded in Luke 11:39–40, Jesus warned about hypocritical externals, "You Pharisees clean the outside of the cup and dish, but inside you are full of greed and wickedness. You foolish people! Did not the one who made the outside make the inside also?" We should take heed.

God sees what is internal. The unseen really matters to him, and we would do well to give it more attention. Whatever external evidence there may be of holiness in our lives, there should be abundantly more beneath the surface. We can't escape this truth with even a cursory look at the New Testament. For instance, in II Timothy 2:20–21, Paul paints this picture:

> *In a large house there are articles not only of gold and silver, but also of wood and clay; some are for special purposes and some for common use. Those who cleanse themselves from the latter will be instruments for special purposes, made holy, useful to the Master and prepared to do any good work.*

God won't force us to clean the sin out of our lives—the stuff in the toilet in a large house. He leaves repentance up to us. But he won't use us for noble purposes unless we are busy repenting, and he will not regard us as holy. So we must deal with the sin in our lives while pursuing holiness. To do that, we need to become familiar with what holiness looks like.

I'm married to a good man. Anyone who knows him would say that about him: "He's a good man." And why would they say that? Because they know of some good things he has done, and they don't know of any egregious harm he has ever caused. He held a steady job for over thirty years, has stayed faithful to the same wife for over fifty years, and has raised a fine family. He's a good man. (I think he's a great man! Good, better, best; great greater, greatest—everything is relative—that's how we think down here.)

It was once naively said of Jesus that he was a "good teacher" (Mark 10:17; Luke 18:18). If the guy who said that had grasped the concept of sinless, perfect, unlimited power, and if that had been what he meant by "good," then he would have been right. What an understatement it was! The guy who said this probably thought he was paying Jesus a compliment. But unless he understood that from a divine perspective "good" equals absolute perfection, it fell so short of what Jesus hoped for the man to conclude that it was practically an insult.

So Jesus helped him out: "No one is good—except God alone" (Mark 10:18; Luke 18:19). What Jesus wanted this guy to see was like a simple mathematical equation (but maybe the guy wasn't good at math). If a=b and c=b, then c=a. If God alone is good, and Jesus is good, then Jesus is God. Jesus wanted this guy to know he was talking to God. The man was not standing before any ordinary or comparatively "good" teacher; he was interacting with God himself!

We are often unfamiliar (and often uncomfortable) with absolutes. We live in a world where almost nothing is absolute. Nothing here is perfectly uncontaminated. So we become satisfied with mostly good. We often accept good intent instead of good behavior, if we think a person means well. Additionally, we lean toward situation ethics and are, therefore, content with allowing circumstances to define right and wrong. This world is saturated with contaminated things, but we call a lot of them "good."

God is good! It's a wild, otherworldly adventure to get acquainted with an absolutely perfect God. Even framing a mental picture of his perfection is mind-blowing. Think of the fruits of his Spirit in terms of perfection (Galatians 5:22–23 ESV):

- perfectly loving
- perfectly joyful
- perfectly peaceful
- perfectly patient
- perfectly kind
- perfectly good
- perfectly faithful

- perfectly gentle
- perfectly self-controlled

I find myself flawed in every area—some more than others. Oh, I *admire* the fruits of God's Spirit. I even aspire to them. But my aim falls far short of perfection. Facing my failure, I am comforted by Paul's admission that he fell short, too:

> *Not that I have already obtained all this, or have already been made perfect, but I press on to take hold of that for which Christ Jesus took hold of me. Brothers and sisters, I do not consider myself yet to have taken hold of it. But one thing I do: Forgetting what is behind and straining toward what is ahead, I press on toward the goal to win the prize for which God has called me heavenward in Christ Jesus. (Philippians 3:12-14)*

When I read about Paul's life, it looks closer to perfection than I could ever imagine achieving (at least after he stopped murdering people!). I would love to reach the level of perfection he did. I want to have his heart. I am so glad the Spirit had him write these words in Philippians. They comfort me in my imperfection and encourage me to keep growing. Paul makes a rather stunning statement right before that about some things he's aiming for:

> *I want to know Christ—yes, to know the power of his resurrection and participate in his sufferings, becoming like him in his death, and so, somehow attaining to the resurrection from the dead. (Philippians 3:10-11)*

Yikes! I think I lack the spirituality to want to suffer and die like Jesus. I mean, I guess if I were facing martyrdom for my faith, I would want to die with Christ's courage and forgiveness toward my killers. And that is really Paul's point. He is not advocating for martyrdom, but for pursuing the character of Christ. God wants us to *experience* Christ's nature, to know him in our very beings. Paul was not longing for martyrdom. He was pursuing the heart and soul of Jesus on the cross, not the cross he was nailed to. What a goal! The thieves who died beside Jesus gave evidence that anybody can be crucified, but only One died with all the fruits of the Spirit on display. Perfect holiness! Jesus' life was holy, and his death was holy.

I think it is easier to repent of outward sins than to change our character and our personality. Crucifying moodiness, selfishness, sarcasm, bitterness, deceitfulness, a critical spirit—those internal sins—is harder in some ways than giving up outward sins. That is why hypocrisy is so easy and so dangerous. We can clean up what people see on the outside and fool them and even deceive ourselves, but God sees the unholy spirit within. And that is what we will give an account for at the judgment. It is not easy to be holy. It takes our deliberate effort and the help of a holy God.

It is easier for me to *do* than to *be*. Life is busy. It gets crowded with lots of stuff. Some of it is really good stuff. I never miss church. I serve in the children's ministry now and then. I share my faith. I contribute to charities. I read my Bible every day—it's a good habit, and I would encourage anyone to do that, but even as I'm writing this, I am reminded of Jesus' warning:

> *"You study the Scriptures diligently because you think that in them you have eternal life. These are the very Scriptures that testify about me, yet you refuse to come to me to have life." (John 5:39-40)*

"Come to me" must have been confusing to his audience.

They probably thought, "We have come to you! We're right here listening to you this moment!" But Jesus meant much more than hanging out with him. He wanted them—and us—to internalize him, to imitate him. The goal of every Christian should be to grow to become as much like Jesus as possible. It is the most glorious pursuit of any lifetime. It was Paul's personal goal, and it was his passion in his ministry:

> *He is the one we proclaim, admonishing and teaching everyone with all wisdom, so that we may present everyone fully mature in Christ. To this end I strenuously contend with all the energy Christ so powerfully works in me. (Colossians 1:28-29)*

There it is: "fully mature in Christ." Being as much like Jesus as time, focus, and our cooperation with the urgings of the Spirit within us can accomplish. Our talents may limit the areas we can serve in and how much we can do, but there is no limit to what we can be. The fruits of God's Spirit (Galatians 5:22–23) are all about being, and what the Bible says about these traits is that "there is no law" restricting them; there are no legal limits. We can have as much of those fruits as we can hold in our natures. We can be loving, joyful, peaceful, and so on, and nobody can tell us we have overdone it! Being these things is the point, yet it seems we give most of our attention to doing rather than to being. If our doing doesn't find its source in what we are, God finds it to have no eternal value.

The Jews were all about doing or not doing. When asked by one of the teachers of the law to tell which command was the most important, Jesus quoted a scripture found in Deuteronomy 6:4–5 with which this man was surely very familiar: "Love the Lord your God with all your heart and with all your soul and with all your mind and with all your strength" (Mark 12:30).

Some scholars suggest that heart, soul, mind, and strength are not separate aspects of our natures, but that they are inseparably intertwined. Maybe so, but we might better assess our own love for God by looking at them individually.

We most often think of loving God or others with our hearts. We can think that loving God emotionally is what really matters, but Jesus is giving equal weight to all four aspects of love. We understand loving God with our strength, because service requires some level of energy. It is a common Christian virtue. Loving God with our mind includes pursuing knowledge about him from his word, as well as controlling the way we think. We are admonished to "take captive every thought to make it obedient to Christ" (II Corinthians 10:5).

Soul is the eternal part of us, the very essence of who we are. It includes our character, our personality. It answers the question, "Who are you?" *Unger's Bible Dictionary* says, "The Hebrew term [soul] may indicate not only the entire inner nature of man, but also his entire personality." Our appearance, our degrees, our bank accounts, our worldly status are irrelevant to God. He cares about our soul, about who we are. He wants us to look like him in our *natures.* Who is God? He is not flesh and blood (except when he came to earth in the person of Jesus). He is spirit, and his Spirit is perfect, holy. His personality and character are righteous. He is righteousness. This is the true destiny for which we were created.

When I first confronted my own personality as compared to the Spirit of God, I was dismayed by the contrast. I had (and still have) many things to change. I was flippant and sarcastic, I loved one-upmanship, I loved arguing, I was easily irritated, I was prideful and a people-pleaser. I had a lot of things to chip away at in my personality. As I pondered whether to become a Christian, one of the hardest things for me was that I actually *liked* these parts of my personality and didn't know who I'd be without them—I thought I would be blah, boring. I thought I'd be giving up my wittiness.

Now I'm finding a new answer to "Who are you?" I am a child of God trying every day to look like him in my character.

God wants to refine us down to the core of who he created us to be. He wants us to be unashamed to look like him. He wants us to value holiness. It is in his image that we will find our greatest contentment and where we'll shine brightest in a dark and desperate world. Loving God with our souls is a lifelong daily process of growth to know him in our very being. It is intentional. Each of us begins at different places with different challenges, but the aim is the same: holiness. We are called to be image bearers of a holy God! That is what will set us apart.

• Meditation •

Call to me and I will answer you and tell you great and unsearchable things you do not know.
— Jeremiah 33:3

Peace through emptying your mind of stress? How about
filling your mind with God? –Anonymous

Chapter 2

Holy Meditation

I remember in the 1960s when meditation was rising in popularity (maybe because of the Beatles) that it was highly controver-
sial among conservative Christians (maybe because of the Beatles).
There was a fear that seeking to empty your mind gave Satan an opportunity to fill it with all manner of ungodly stuff. That fear died
down, and the health benefits of relaxation techniques began to be
charted. Meditation entered a period of mainstream acceptance—
and the growing popularity of Yoga didn't hurt! (Well, it hurt every
ligament in my body when I tried it. But it didn't hurt the popularity
of meditation.)

Meditation has been given little attention as a Christian practice. Passing decades have popularized focused breathing as meditation—slowly count as you inhale, slowly count as you exhale,
mindful all the time of posture and tempo. Its benefits are written
about in magazines and medical journals. It calms the mind, lowers
blood pressure, oxygenates the brain, and sharpens thinking. But
this barely resembles the meditation recommended in the Bible.

Meditation as a common Christian discipline still doesn't
seem to have caught on. God didn't exactly command us to meditate, but he certainly advocated for it and attached promises of
great benefit to it. David mentioned eight times in Psalm 119 that
he meditated on God's word. When God was instructing Joshua

how to approach his role as Israel's new leader, he told him this: "Keep this Book of the Law always on your lips; meditate on it day and night" (Joshua 1:8). Every page of the Bible is an exposure of the heart of God. Filling our minds with his word is the only way to get his heart into our hearts.

God promises good things for the one who meditates on his word. "Blessed is the one...whose delight is in the law of the Lord, and who meditates on his law day and night" (Psalm 1:1–2). The promise of blessings for meditation should provide ample motivation to learn how to practice it. Those blessings may differ from person to person, and some may be surprising, but they are worth looking for because God always keeps his promises.

In Psalm 119, David's mention of meditating on God's word is in verses 15, 23, 27, 48, 78, 97, 99, and 148. David surely had enough time for meditation, since he spent week after week out alone with a bunch of sheep. There he could think deeply about something, and he chose to have that something be Scripture: "I have hidden your word in my heart that I might not sin against you" (Psalm 119:11). While meditation didn't prove to be an impenetrable barrier against sin in David's life, his heart longing must have touched the heart of God.

Most of us don't have the luxury of such long stretches of uninterrupted thought on God. But sadly, we often fail to plan five or ten minutes into our days for meditation. Oh, we read our Bibles. Some of us even memorize verses, and that certainly qualifies as meditation. But wouldn't it be amazing if it were such a common practice among us that we shared those meditation experiences or often asked each other, "So, what did you meditate on this week?"

David's goal was that his very thoughts, not just his actions, would please God (Psalm 104:34). He invited God to examine his thinking and help him see his internal life more clearly and change anything that didn't please him:

> Search me, God, and know my heart;
>   test me and know my anxious thoughts.
> See if there is any offensive way in me,
>   and lead me in the way everlasting. (Psalm 139:23-24)

He meditated on God's love (Psalm 48:9), on God's law (Psalm 119:15), on God's wonders (Psalm 119:27), and on God's promises (Psalm 119:148). David asked for God's help to shape his thoughts: "May these words of my mouth and this meditation of my heart be pleasing in your sight, Lord, my Rock and my Redeemer" (Psalm 19:14).

With David's heart and mind so full of all things God, it is little wonder that God called him "a man after my own heart" (Acts 13:22). David and God thought about the same things. They had a heart connection because they remained on the same wavelength. They shared a passion for righteousness. David loved everything about God.

Some days I think I try harder to avoid sinful thinking—lustful thoughts, greedy thoughts, or vengeful thoughts—than to focus my efforts on thinking righteous thoughts pleasing to God, to "take captive every thought to make it obedient to Christ" (II Corinthians 10:5). Maybe it was easier for David without a daily dose of newspaper headlines, numbing televised vapidness, or the demands and stresses of the workplace. There are so many distracting irritations Satan can put in our paths (Ephesians 6:12). Perhaps Scripture meditation is a weapon we should employ instead of giving Satan so many opportunities for victory in the battle for our minds. After all, it was Scripture that Jesus used to send Satan off when he was confronted with temptation (Matthew 4:1–11).

In the chaos of life's demands, it can feel like a stretch to set aside ten or fifteen minutes (in addition to whatever time we spend in prayer and Bible study) to quiet our minds, forget our to-do lists, and refuse to think of meditation as just another thing on that to-do list. It is sad to use prayer as a catalog of wishes or demands instead of an intimate time of awestruck love. Even thanking God for specific blessings, while this is a valuable habit, is no substitute for being still and meditating on his wonderfulness. It is not just his blessings that are wonderful; it's him!

Scripture meditation is holy because it is set apart from every other kind of meditation. Its source is set apart, its practice is set apart, and its impact is set apart by what it accomplishes in the human heart.

Try sitting and whispering a phrase or verse from Scripture and watch your mind be transformed (Romans 12:2). See your understanding of Scripture expand, and your attitudes, moods, and interactions improve. Meditation can focus your goals for changing your natural tendencies to godly tendencies. Here is an example of a verse worth repeating as meditation:

> *To him who loves us and has freed us from our sins by his blood...-to him be glory and power for ever and ever! Amen. (Revelation 1:5-6)*

Certainly, passionate prayers must be included in every Christian's repertoire along with praise and thanksgiving, and simple conversations with God as a friend. "During the days of Jesus' life on earth, he offered up prayers and petitions with fervent cries and tears" (Hebrews 5:7). Jesus offers us powerful examples of uninhibited, emotionally expressive prayers. Somehow, quite sadly, many Christians have become bored with their prayer life because their

prayers have no variation and have settled into an insipid same-
ness. We are the only ones who can invest in our prayer and meditation habits to keep them worthy of the attention of an awesome
God. It seems that most of us lean toward certain styles of prayer,
and if those styles don't include meditative prayer, I hope this book
will encourage that broader, multidimensional communication
with God.

Since Scripture doesn't give specific mandates for the methods of meditation, we can craft it to fit our very own personal relationship with God. Any scripture we choose can become our perfect "mantra." We can close our eyes and repeat a passage until it is
memorized. We can gaze at nature and marvel at our Creator. We
can whisper praise on our knees. We can mentally embrace a truth
about God and bow our spirits in humility. We can delight in one of
his promises. We can choose a line from a favorite hymn to sing or
chant. We can do any of these things or use other methods, but the
idea is to focus uninterrupted for a period of time, increasing that
time as we grow accustomed to that special kind of stillness and
feel its transformative effects.

He says, "Be still and know that I am God;
  I will be exalted among the nations.
  I will be exalted in the earth." (Psalm 46:10-11)

Meditation is a way of answering God's plea that we "be still."
He knows our need for a quieted mind saturated with thoughts of
him. It is at once reassuring, empowering, hopeful, awe-inspiring,
humbling, and incredibly intimate. It is an intimacy God longs to
have with us and one that we desperately need—although we are
sometimes oblivious to that need.

I hope, if it's not already, that meditation will become a delightfully anticipated part of your day. I hope this little book benefits your quest to be holy. To that end, use the suggested scripture for meditation at the close of each chapter as a starting point to craft your own meditation customs. Be holy. Set yourself apart in a deeper relationship with God your Father. Saturate yourself with his heart and desires.

• Meditation •

Keep this Book of the Law always on your lips.
— Joshua 1:8

> Jesus...sees who we're becoming, and he wants us
> to become love.   –Bob Goff

Chapter 3

Holy Love

In his thought-provoking book of the same title, Francis Chan calls God's love "crazy love." And in a popular contemporary Christian song, God's love is called reckless. Crazy, reckless—human vocabulary trying to describe the love of God. His love is both those things and so much more.

I remember contemplating the line from an old hymn that says he "has bought us and sought us and guided our ways" and trying to figure out whether the order was accurate (silly me—I do things like that). I realized it was astoundingly correct.

First, God bought us at the incalculable price of his own Son's blood.

Second, he sought us. This is the astounding part—after paying such a high price for us, he didn't take possession, but rather honored our free will to respond! I can't imagine paying for a Tesla and then giving it permission to decide whether to let me drive it.

Third, if we do respond to his purchase of us, he guides our ways. He doesn't guide us just with directives from the Bible. He personally stays with each of us, caring about every aspect of our lives: reading our every thought, weeping when we weep (and often when we don't, but should, as when we grieve his Holy Spirit), rejoicing with us over victories large and small, forgiving, forgiving,

forgiving, in constant contact, walking beside us through every event of our days, and just a prayer away. Because of his love for us, he longs for us to accept his guidance because he has our very best interests at heart and knows the way we should go. This is not an ego-driven God who dictates obedience. His immeasurable love wants the absolute best for us.

It is not just that God is loving, which is demonstrated repeatedly in the pages of the Bible and in our lives. It is this: God *is* love! GOD IS LOVE. It's a mind-blowing truth. It sums up everything about his character, his Spirit. And everything about every aspect of his character springs from that core quality of who he is—love. We'll look at a few of those qualities on these pages, beginning with the fruits of his Spirit.

It is hard for us to imagine when we are grieving a tragic loss in our lives that we remain in the center of God's love. When we look at war and natural disasters, we are also prone to question the love of God, but with every unpredictable and destabilizing event on earth, the love of God is the one dependable constant. The Apostle Paul understood this, and God had him reassure us in Romans 8:38–39 that nothing can separate us from the love of God—not death, not demons, not now, not ever, no matter what, we can count on the love of God. It will surround us and infuse us, and it does not depend on our being able to feel it. Its comfort only depends on us knowing it by faith.

It is a daunting task to try to capture in words the love of God, and much better writers and scholars than I have tried. It truly is tackling an impossible job. It is unlikely we even have sufficient adjectives and adverbs to shed light on God's love. It takes so much more than words; it takes every revelation in the Bible plus faith. I am amused by Paul telling the Ephesian church that he was praying for them to *know* God's *unknowable* love:

And I pray that you, being rooted and established in love, may have power, together with all the Lord's holy people, to grasp how wide and long and high and deep is the love of Christ, and to know this love that surpasses knowledge. (Ephesians 3:17-19)

Worthy of note in that passage is the idea that it takes power to grasp God's love. It is not some simple concept. We'll need help. God offers that help through his indwelling Spirit, but we must pray for understanding and a powerful faith to fathom even a portion of its meaning. It takes a mighty trust in God to interpret life events through his unfailing love, especially when those events seem to contradict our own ideas of what love should look like.

The vastness of God's love is immeasurable. Nothing in our life can reach beyond it. Think of outer space, beyond our galaxy; think of floating in it and trying to reach its borders. It's silly. We know next to nothing about the scope of the universe even though brilliant astronomers have written awe-inspiring documents. These writings are perhaps our best hope of understanding the immensity of God's love. The boundlessness of space is a great metaphor for God's love, which has a purity and magnitude that has no equivalent.

Of course, the best author to ever write about the love of God was his own Spirit. Through the Apostle Paul, God offers a definition of love by breaking down its separate elements in I Corinthians 13. It is a passage so beautiful, so familiar, and so prized that even unbelievers have it framed and hanging on their walls. It exposes the intertwined pieces of love, revealing that love is patient, kind, not envious, not boastful, not proud, not disrespectful, not self-seeking, not easily angered, and more besides. And I have a hunch it is not an exhaustive list, but all God thought we could handle! This is who God is—*this* love. It is a completely selfless and sacrificial love. To say that God's love is holy, that it sets him apart, is a gross understatement. With each other, when we are at our best, we experience only bits of it.

A sweet and love-defining memory stands out for me that helps me understand it. While my husband was out of town, our youngest son had to be hospitalized with an intestinal disorder, and the local doctors were stumped. After a day or so they sent me to pack a bag and return to follow an ambulance to Children's Hospital. Feeling alone because of Ron's absence, filled with sadness over Matt's suffering and anxiety about a prognosis, I arrived home to find my friend, Lynda, cleaning my house. I greeted her briefly and hurried to my bedroom to shower, change, and pack. In the process of this preparation, I wondered why Lynda's cleaning meant so much to me when my son's well-being held such priority in my heart that I really didn't care if the house burned down, much less if it were clean. It struck me with sudden intensity that it was Lynda's demonstration of love that offered me unmatched comfort. As Bob Goff says in his wonderful book of the same title, "love does." And Lynda "did"! Lynda couldn't make Matt well (God did that), but her "doing" communicated a blessing to me that nothing else could have. Love has miraculous effects.

God sees beneath the surface. He sees every motive of our hearts. He knows whether we perform out of pride or duty or love. He is only impressed by love. Jesus said, "I know you. I know that you do not have the love of God in your hearts" (John 5:42). With great compassion, he also knows that we are only dust (Psalm 103:14). He stands eager to help us to increasingly comprehend his love and to offer that love to those around us.

The Bible says God has given each of us different gifts. Romans 12:6–8 tells us that these gifts include prophesying, serving, teaching, encouraging, giving, leading, and showing mercy. View those gifts through the warning in I Corinthians 13:1–3, and it puts love and action into perspective: actions, even the most sacrificial and religious ones, count for nothing without love! They may benefit someone, and they may make us look good, but God finds them worthless to our account unless they come from love.

There are no limits to the ways in which God can show love, but we are limited. Still, we are not without ways of loving. Looking to the gifts he has given us is a way of discerning how we might be most effective in showing the love of God. Regarding this discernment, consider Paul's prayer for the Philippian church:

And this is my prayer: that your love may abound more and more in knowledge and depth of insight, so that you may be able to discern what is best and may be pure and blameless for the day of Christ, filled with the fruit of righteousness that comes through Jesus Christ—to the glory and praise of God. (Philippians 1:9-11)

We may easily accept that God's compassion and mercy come from love, but we have a harder time with his wrath or justice having love as their source. We live in a world that has pitifully misdefined love. It seems that the world's strident cry is that tolerance (of sin in particular) is love's highest standard. But real love would never tolerate things that are destructive to our souls. God's love as revealed in the Bible set a moral standard. Love is the beginning of God's story; love is the end of the story; love is the story itself.

And love is something more than all its elements—
a palpitating, sensitive, living thing. –Henry Drummond

Embracing the love of God, as you experience it and as you offer it to others, is life's highest calling and greatest satisfaction. We are tiny specks in a vast sea of love. We need to learn how to understand all that we can of it, how to delight in it, and how to overflow with it to bless every life around us. Mother Teresa once said, "I am a little pencil in the hand of a writing God who is sending a love letter to the world." The Bible has been called a love letter from God, and we are privileged to become the living evidence of his love.

Love is our purpose in this world. It's all that really matters (Galatians 5:6). Aristotle taught that you could only love those who deserved to be loved. God forbid that we should set ourselves up as judges of who deserves to be loved! Jesus told us to love even our enemies (Matthew 5:44), and he fully demonstrated what that looks like when he walked on this earth. God recorded Jesus' example so we could imitate it, and he told us to "walk in the way of love" just as Jesus did (Ephesians 5:1–2). This is the highest calling. The closer we come to imitating Jesus, the more we are set apart, the more we are holy.

Imitation is a great place to start, but as we imitate, God shapes us into his image from the inside out. That is why "God's love has been poured out into our hearts through the Holy Spirit, who has been given to us" (Romans 5:5). That love was put into us by God! It's right there! We just have to access it, nurture it, and use it to bless others, and God will make it grow. We experience God's love, therefore "we love because he first loved us" (I John 4:19). Without God's love there would be no love at all, anywhere, ever.

A practical definition of love that really resonated with me is one that Gary Francis wrote in *Temperatures of the Soul:* "Love is to give at the expense of self to benefit others." Love will always cost us something. It will cost time or effort or money or embarrassment or pain or vulnerability or lots of other stuff, and maybe all of the above, but it will cost! Accepting that fact should cause us to see sacrifice differently and even to look for opportunities to pour ourselves out.

The feeling of love is invisible, but its fruits are not. You can always see the fruits of love. This is important for many reasons. One that Jesus highlighted was that it is through our love that "everyone will know" we are disciples of his. Love is the evidence of belonging to Jesus, of being set apart (John 13:35). We are told, "Be devoted to one another in love. Honor one another above yourselves" (Romans 12:10). Now, there's a competition the world doesn't often engage in!

Our being loving is so significant to God that Jesus said love was the most important command (Matthew 22:34–40). In Romans 13:8–10, we are taught that love fulfills the intent behind every item in the ten commandments. They are all about how to love God and how to love people. While they are commandments that belong to an old testament that has been replaced by a new law, love fulfills Christ's law too (Galatians 6:2). We are taught in Paul's letter to the Corinthian church that love is the greatest thing in the world—greater even than faith and hope (I Corinthians 13:13). It is impossible to overestimate the need to increasingly understand God's love and grow in living a life of love (Ephesians 5:1–2).

The impact of love is miraculous. Everything about the nature of God invites our imitation, but in a list of some of his qualities—compassion, kindness, humility, gentleness, patience, and forgiveness—God makes his priority clear: "And over all these virtues put on love, which binds them all together in perfect unity" (Colossians 3:13–14). His appeal here refers to the concept of holiness in verse 12: "Therefore, as God's chosen people, holy and dearly loved..." We must aim for a set-apart love. Our holiness, our set-apartness, finds its most lofty and impacting expressions in love, so we need

34

to make sure love is expressed.

We also need to make sure it's real! God cannot be fooled by hypocrisy. Real love is selfless. To whatever extent we can set aside self-interest to put the needs of others above our own, it is a set-apart way of thinking and a set-apart way of living. Getting nothing in return is irrelevant to the decision to love.

> Love expressed in action is never wasted. Even when it's not reciprocated, loving someone like Christ is never pointless. It is not something to regret. At a minimum, Christ counts it as love expressed to him. —Jana Lusk

Every negative or sinful tendency within us faces defeat when we love. We can't be critical or hateful or grouchy or prejudiced or bitter when we really love. God is ever vigilant in his search to find love in our hearts. It is the premier connective fiber between our hearts and his. With love as the supreme summary of the nature of God, we will continue to examine aspects of his holy, loving character.

• Meditation •

Perhaps something in this chapter or in your experience is essential for you to ponder right now. Concentrate on the love of God.

Within your temple, O God, we meditate on your unfailing love.
—Psalm 48:9

I sometimes wonder whether all pleasures are
a substitute for joy. —C.S. Lewis

Chapter 4

Holy Joy

It is a mysterious joy that God's Spirit places within us. It can make tortured prisoners chained in a miserable jail cell sing hymns (Acts 16:25). That certainly speaks of a joy outside of circumstances! Set-apart joy is not fragile. It is dependable, always accessible, but not always evident on the surface.

This joy doesn't tamp down other emotions. It accepts cohabitation with sorrow, fear, and grief. It challenges the emotions of anger and resentment, making us face our own fallen state and desperate need for holiness and the help of God. Some may hope that denial of unpleasant realities will make joy accessible. Joy never requires denial, but in facing reality, it claims an unchallenged place in our hearts. Proverbs 14:13 tells us that "even in laughter the heart may ache."

After the shock of an earthquake and a conversation with an angel whose appearance was like lightning, the women who first found Jesus' empty tomb certainly experienced a flood of emotions. "So the women hurried away from the tomb, afraid yet filled with joy, and ran to tell his disciples" (Matthew 28:8). Fear and joy at the same time.

We are not promised that we will never suffer affliction. God promises his presence, his comfort, and his compassion (Isaiah 49:13). Instead of promising ease and prosperity, Jesus promised, "In this world you will have trouble. But take heart! I have overcome the world" (John 16:33). Count on it—we will have trouble in this life. We may wish for different, visible evidence that Jesus has overcome the world, but he's calling us to a new way of thinking.

I was blessed to witness this beautiful, irrational joy in my friend, Gloria Baird. Her joy was always a hallmark of her personality, but it was most stunning as she was facing imminent death. I asked her husband, Al, to write his thoughts on her joy at the end.

> Hard times are inevitable. Among our hardest was the loss of three babies. And the hardest of all was Gloria's six-year battle with cancer, which finally took her from me. As hard as those years were, Gloria was continually full of joy. One of her favorite verses was Psalm 31:14: 'You are my God. My times are in your hands.' That was the philosophy she lived by—regardless of how hard the circumstances were, God was in control and had her in the palm of his hand.
>
> Her final days were probably her most joyful. We came back from her oncologist appointment with the news that the cancer had spread to her brain and that she probably had "weeks rather than months" left. To say that it was not a happy time for either of us would be a gross understatement; but her joy never changed. I found a text later that she had sent to some friends: "Dr says he thinks I have weeks not months... so Heaven here I come!!!! Don't like saying goodbye!!! Love you so much! Keep fighting the fight!!" Twelve days later she was gone. Heaven was her ultimate destination—mission accomplished! How can anyone find more joy than that?

The author of Psalm 43 beautifully expresses the conflicted emotions that accompany hardship. He felt rejected by God, yet called God his "stronghold." He speaks of mourning and oppression, yet acknowledges that God is faithful and calls him "my joy and my delight." He searches introspectively, asking, "Why my soul, are you downcast?" Finally, with wise self-talk, he counsels himself, "Put your hope in God."

To fight through doubt and despair often requires facing our own contradictory and faithless emotions and taking them to God. Instead of turning away from God in shame when we see our own hearts, it is a call to turn to him. David prayed, "Bring joy to your servant, Lord, for I put my trust in you" (Psalm 86:4). We can't trust ourselves to change our own hearts, but so often we try. My friend Lin once observed, "We try to get the strength to go to God instead of going to God for the strength." God is the supplier of every good thing in our hearts and lives, including a kind of joy the world cannot comprehend.

The joy of the LORD is your strength. (Nehemiah 8:10)

No matter the awful circumstances life throws at us, our joy in the Lord will supply the strength to endure. The reasons for joy offered by God are numerous. Foremost is God himself. My prayers often begin with thanking God for the wonder of all that he is: perfect, righteous, holy, just, loving, powerful, and more. I am amazed, in awe, delighted!

God has made every provision for our joy—the beauty of his creation, the Word, his faithfulness, his love. If we don't feel joy when we ponder these gifts, we need to understand our own hearts and search out the reasons we are unable to allow joy to eclipse negative emotions. Perhaps pain or loss have overshadowed joy as we typically define it. Practicing a life of joy is like any other trait of God that he hopes we will embody. It takes prayer and a focused effort and will become more natural, even habitual, over time as God transforms our hearts.

That indescribable, mysterious joy has many heavenly sources. Both Psalm 16:11 and Psalm 21:6 say there is joy in the presence of God. Only faith can comprehend his presence, but it is a reality we need to be aware of every minute. What a joy to know that whatever our day holds, God is right there beside us. When Jesus was leaving his disciples just before his ascension, he promised he would be with them always (Matthew 28:20). It is a promise of companionship we desperately need.

The deeds of God bring joy. Every page in the Bible tells of the wonderful, amazing, inspiring things that he has done. And he has not stopped—his deeds are always present; he is always at work in our lives. We just need the eyes to see them.

> For you make me glad by your deeds, LORD;
>   I sing for joy at what your hands have done. (Psalm 92:4)

> The whole earth is filled with awe at your wonders;...
>   you call forth songs of joy. (Psalm 65:8)

Every verse in Psalm 119 (and there are 176 of them!) praises the words of God, the laws of God, his statutes: "Your statutes are my heritage forever; they are the joy of my heart" (Psalm 119:111). If the Bible is uninteresting to you or somehow burdensome, it is time to beg God for a different perspective. God's word was designed by him to expose his heart and his will and to help us understand our own hearts. We should be fascinated. We need to stand in grateful awe and rejoice. Jeremiah said God's words were his heart's delight (Jeremiah 15:16).

The precepts of the LORD are right,
  giving joy to the heart. (Psalm 19:8)

God's love is a supreme and precious source of joy. Just waking up to a new day and knowing it is a gift of God's love is worth rejoicing over. He has demonstrated and proven his love in multiple ways, but certainly, providing our salvation through the death of his only Son is the greatest and most stunning evidence (John 3:16). Looking at things that make us happy on earth is an unreliable measure of God's love, though they are often gifts from him. But the cross should reign above all and put everything else in perspective.

Satisfy us in the morning with your unfailing love,
  that we may sing for joy and be glad all our days. (Psalm 90:14)

The kingdom of heaven is a treasure and should be a source of great joy. Jesus told a parable of a man who found a treasure and hid it and "then in his joy" sold everything he had in order to buy it (Matthew 13:44). The message is plain: the kingdom is so precious that it should be a joy to make any sacrifice to have it for our own. Our attitudes about God's kingdom here on earth can be most contrary to joy. Oh, we look forward to a heavenly kingdom, but we can have all sorts of disgruntled attitudes about the church. We can become ungrateful, unhappy, opinionated evaluators and critics of function, leaders, and one another—the things that God intended for our joy.

Some joy is quiet and personal. Some is exuberant and rowdy. God likes both. The Bible speaks of shouting, clapping, and leaping for joy. It also talks of singing for joy. I am not musically skilled, but I am grateful for the brothers and sisters who are and who offer their talents to the corporate worship services. They bless my own worship experience.

> *Sing to him a new song;*
> *play skillfully, and shout for joy.* (Psalm 33:3)

> *Clap your hands, all you nations;*
> *shout to God with cries of joy.* (Psalm 47:1)

When I think of my own failures and sins, I can plunge into dark regret. I am stunned by the forgiveness of God. It doesn't make any sense. But it makes me want to run into God's arms crying for joy. There is no greater reason for joy, no matter what sorrows exist.

> *"I have swept away your offenses like a cloud,*
> *your sins like the morning mist."* (Isaiah 44:22-23)

We have been delivered from damnation! This well recommends singing for joy when we are alone spending time with God as well as when we come to assemble with the church. We should not come to church just to be led in worship, but to bring our worship to combine in joy with God's family. We all have countless reasons to rejoice separately and together.

> *My lips will shout for joy*
> *when I sing praise to you—*
> *I whom you have delivered.* (Psalm 71:23)

Peter praised the scattered and persecuted disciples for exhibiting an "inexpressible and glorious joy." What an exquisite description of the joy God holds out to us. The reason they were able to have joy in the face of great losses and ever-present threats was because their hearts were more invested in heaven and salvation than in comfort and earthly gain. It's that focus on having attained the final prize, the highest goal—salvation—that is the best source of a Christian's joy.

Though you have not seen him, you love him; and even thought you do not see him now, you believe in him and are filled with an inexpressible and glorious joy, for you are receiving the end result of your faith, the salvation of your souls. (I Peter 1:8-9)

When I read through the New Testament, it seems to me that the early disciples had a more urgent focus on heaven compared to the relaxed anticipation I see among Christians today, myself included. The prospect of heaven should be an amazing source of hope and joy. Peter cautioned (or promised) "the end of all things is near" (I Peter 4:7). That was around 2000 years ago. Certainly, the end is nearer now as we reckon time, yet the joy of heaven seems diminished by the effort to find joy on earth. I hope it doesn't take suffering and persecution for us to long for heaven. God described heaven for us in as much detail as we could comprehend, but it remains largely a glorious mystery. Trusting God makes us believe that heaven is bliss beyond compare. Heaven—what we can understand of it—should fill us with great joy. But it will likely require some deliberate dreaming about it.

Amazingly, we are the source of God's joy! We are the "apple of [his] eye" (Psalm 17:8). He has engraved us on the palms of his hands (Isaiah 49:16). It is stunning that we hold such a place in his heart. He spared nothing to call us his own and make us heirs of all he has to offer (Romans 8:32).

For the LORD takes delight in his people;...
Let his faithful people delight in this honor
and sing for joy. (Psalm 149:4-5)

• Meditation •

As you read this chapter, you may have thought of a scripture that warrants your meditation. In lieu of that, perhaps mentally repeating the scripture below will be a blessing to you.

Oh, how I love your law! I meditate on it all day long.
—Psalm 119:97

If we have not peace within ourselves, it is in vain to seek it from outward sources. —Francis de La Rochefoucaulds

Chapter 5

Holy Peace

There is that familiar cliché about beautiful but vapid beauty pageant contestants wishing for world peace. We all wish for it, but it is the epitome of wishful thinking. From the moment sin entered the world, peace became illusive. Innocent people are affected in devastating ways. External, worldwide peace will never exist. Personal, internal peace is threatened by events ranging from minor inconveniences to terrorism, tsunamis, disease, poverty, starvation, earthquakes, floods, and wildfires. It is in these varied and complex events that God steps in to offer peace.

Paramount in the Christian's understanding is faith in the bedrock of our peace: we have peace with God. What makes us value that holy peace is a deep, humble awareness that we were once God's enemies (Romans 5:10). Immersing ourselves in an eternal perspective keeps us on an even keel in an unstable and unpredictable world. Peace with God should hold a holy precedence in our hearts. It puts outward stressors and our own natures—whether calm or excitable—under an umbrella of truth that allows us to find real peace.

*Since we have been justified through faith, we have peace
with God through our Lord Jesus Christ.* (Romans 5:1)

Peace is priceless! It cost God everything. It cost Jesus torturous suffering and a humiliating death (Isaiah 53:5). Jesus bought peace with God for us when he paid the debt we owed because of our sin. It is an amazing truth to contemplate. Without God revealing it, I would not have known that there was no solution for the terrible consequence of my sin—death. It is agony and ecstasy. I am responsible for Jesus' death and I hate that, but I'm ecstatic about the gifts his death bought for me: forgiveness, a relationship with God, a spiritual family, eternal life, peace! We have "peace through his blood, shed on the cross" (Colossians 1:20).

Peace with God! Lean into it; meditate on it; pray grateful prayers about it; believe it; rejoice in it. This is the peace that matters. This peace is the foundation of any other peace we hope to attain. Jesus didn't just buy us peace, "he himself is our peace" (Ephesians 2:14).

Satan, the enemy of our souls, wants to annihilate our peace. He wants to keep us in a constant state of anxiety, worry, fear and doubt. He wants us to believe that escape through temporary pleasures is a way to find peace. He creates havoc in the world and hopes we'll blame God; that way, he can rob us of our only source of lasting peace. He wants to threaten our confidence in the promises of God and in our salvation. We deny Satan this power by grounding ourselves in the word of God. We are at war with Satan, but God has equipped us with effective armor; it is just up to us to put it on (Ephesians 6:10–17).

Satan has lots of schemes to rob us of peace. We are aware of external ones and less aware of the internal. For example, there is greed. The endless quest for more is exhausting. Greed wars against contentment. Proverbs 14:30 tells us that "a heart at peace gives life to the body, but envy rots the bones." Doctors today have become increasingly aware that mental, spiritual, and physical health are linked, but there is no pharmaceutical answer for true peace.

Another ploy of Satan is false doctrine. Jeremiah warned about the bogus security to be found in false teachings. "They dress the wound of my people as though it were not serious. 'Peace, peace,' they say when there is no peace" (Jeremiah 6:14, 8:11). We are easy prey for teachings proclaiming that there are low standards for receiving God's grace, or that he grades on a curve and we are not as bad as the next guy. So Satan, when he can't keep us agitated, offers us a false peace. On one end or the other, he's got us!

When Gideon was called to rescue Israel from the oppression of the Midianites, he was frightened and felt inadequate. He built an altar and named it The Lord Is Peace (Judges 6:24). But he still had to go to war. Sometimes, even though we have eternal peace with God, we have to fight for peace in our day-to-day lives. Even though the spiritual battle rages, we are never alone in this battle; we are only called to trust and be still (Exodus 14:14; Psalm 37:7, 46:10). Maybe we need to build an altar that we can call The Lord Is Peace as some visible, tangible reminder of who God is. I am not advocating ancient altar-building; a sticky note might do, or a song we sing every day, a scripture that we have committed to memory, or praying continually (I Thessalonians 5:17).

> Now may the Lord of peace himself give you peace at all times and in every way. The Lord be with you all. (II Thessalonians 3:16)

So the Lord is the source of our peace, but do we play a role, and what exactly is our role in experiencing it? The Bible gives us several tools for accessing an unassailable peace.

1. Seek it. Pursue it. (Psalm 34:14; I Peter 3:10–11)

2. Ask God for it. (II Thessalonians 3:16; Psalm 29:11)

3. Live in it. (Colossians 3:15)

4. Make every effort. (II Peter 3:14; Romans 14:19)

5. Study it. Look for examples of peace in others to imitate. (Philippians 4:9; Isaiah 48:18)

6. Practice it. (Romans 12:18, 14:19; James 3:18; Matthew 5:9)

7. Cling to it in Scripture. (Psalm 119:165)

8. Grow your trust in God. Invest your thoughts in it. (Isaiah 26:3; Romans 8:6–8)

9. Be righteous. (Isaiah 32:17)

10. Be a peacemaker. (James 3:18)

There is no better way to be a peacemaker than to offer the peace you have to others. It is wonderful if the peace you have is so visible and appealing that others notice and inquire. Since peace has companions, that could happen. Romans 14:17 says that peace is accompanied by righteousness and joy; Romans 15:13 says its companions are hope, joy and trust; Isaiah 32:17 tells us that peace goes along with quietness and confidence; Colossians 3:15 joins peace with gratitude; Jude 2 couples it with mercy and love. These are all qualities everyone longs for: righteousness, love, joy, hope, trust, quietness, confidence, and a heart full of gratitude. Peace not only blesses us, but also everyone around us. Jesus said, "Blessed are the peacemakers, for they will be called children of God"

(Matthew 5:9).

Unfortunately, there are many things that assault our peace. Life is unpredictable. We have little control over external chaos. Consider Job suffering unthinkable losses. No wonder he said, "I have no peace, no quietness; I have no rest, but only turmoil" (Job 3:26). But Job's trust in God remained steadfast even when he was questioning why God had allowed such pain. The Apostle Paul was not unaffected by anxiety. He had "no peace of mind" when he couldn't find Titus (II Corinthians 2:13). He was distressed over Epaphroditus' illness and feared that his friend might die (Philippians 2:25–28).

Okay, full disclosure here. I would feel hypocritical if I didn't add this confession. I had almost finished this chapter when all the work I had done disappeared (at least as far as my limited computer skills could discern). I am a slow writer, and I'm writing with a deadline. I broke down in tears. I prayed, "God, is this a sign that you don't want me to write this book?" I was trying to be okay, to find peace. But my daughter Meredith was in town from Denver. I just told her my sadness. I knew she has a responsible job, but I didn't know that she is a computer whiz. She not only retrieved all that I thought was lost but adjusted several other annoying issues with my laptop. Anyway, while writing a chapter on peace, I lost mine! By nature, I'm excitable. I'm calm most of the time, but I am irrepressibly gleeful with good news and a puddle of tears with bad news.

I know how to do the work. It starts with prayer. There would have been lots more prayers required if Meredith had not come to my rescue. If I'd had to abort this book, I would have needed to offload my frustration with a compassionate friend. And pray. And pray. I know I would have come to peaceful resolution in the end. I just thought I should let you know that I understand the struggle with peace versus panic—even over little things.

Jesus understands the struggle, too. In Gethsemane, he fought for peace, for resolution with the will of God (Matthew 26:36–46). He didn't want to face the kind of death he was going to die. He wasn't obsessing on irrational fears. He knew exactly what he was facing—public humiliation, torture, separation from the Father, death. But he did the work. He openly confessed his great sorrow and dread. He pleaded for God to find another way, an alternate plan. Finally, he peacefully surrendered to the will of the Father. Jesus' work toward peace in Gethsemane is an extreme example. Most of us will face minor threats to our peace compared to this, unless we become martyrs. But by facing the most extreme attack on peaceful surrender to horrible circumstances, we can always know that no matter how great our sorrow and terrible our crisis, Jesus understands.

Holy peace is most appealing, and we feel our greatest need for it amid turmoil—and it is an unstable and chaotic world we live in. We have little control over external peace. In Jesus' final days on earth, he promised his disciples (and us) in John 14:27, "Peace I leave with you; my peace I give you. I do not give to you as the world gives." That's the TRUTH! His peace is not what the world offers. It doesn't even make sense to the world. Paul told the Philippians, "The peace of God, which transcends all understanding, will guard your hearts and minds in Christ Jesus" (Philippians 4:7). In this same passage, Paul says to ask for what you need and give thanks. Holy peace is completely dependent on God.

It seems contradictory that the Prince of Peace (Isaiah 9:6) promises: "Do not suppose that I have come to bring peace to the earth. I did not come to bring peace, but a sword" (Matthew 10:34; Luke 12:51). The cross is our surest example of the fight we volunteer to engage in when we become Christians. Our faith may create resentment and conflict—even accusations and threats—in the hearts and behavior of those who disagree with how we live it (I Peter 4:4). That divide can be very painful for us. While God always wants us to try to have peace with everyone, we cannot control the attitudes of others (Hebrews 12:14). Our only hope for peace in those circumstances is a steadfast trust in God.

Peace takes work. It takes practice and grows with use. Peace makes you strong (Psalm 29:11). It makes you resilient. It gives you courage. It will straighten your back, and it is better for your posture than Yoga. It makes you draw near to God.

• Meditation •

Better a dry crust of bread with peace and quiet than a house full of feasting, with strife.
— Proverbs 17:1

You have to have a lot of patience to learn patience.
–Stanislaw J. Lec

Chapter 6

Holy Patience

People are occasionally described as having the "patience of Job." The phrase loses its meaning when applied to someone enduring temporary inconveniences. I think Job might be chagrinned to know that, for instance, an eye-rolling parent tolerating the misbehavior of a child gets credited with the kind of patience he exhibited.

When the Bible talks about patience, it does not speak in terms of gutting it out through some petty annoyance. It points to persevering in righteousness despite terrible suffering. Often it is hard for us to remain righteously patient waiting in long lines or stuck in traffic. Without a righteous perspective, we can experience misery in minor issues, and we can make everyone around us miserable, too.

We are drawn to patient people. There is appealing wisdom in patience—probably because wisdom is the source of patience. As Proverbs 19:11 says, "a person's wisdom yields patience." It is a gift when a calm and quiet spirit comes naturally to a person. Perhaps they get a head start on developing the wisdom of holy patience. But all of us have to start somewhere. Whatever our personalities, we are called to the same righteous composure. Romans 12:12 states it as a command: "Be joyful in hope, patient in affliction, faithful in prayer." Just do it. Begin where you are and grow.

I often hear friends admitting that they struggle with impatience. Me too. That confession is often met with sympathy, and that is appropriate, but such an admission should not be brushed aside as trivial. Every occasion when we face pain, disappointment, or frustration is an opportunity to grow. I just wonder whether, because impatience is such a common shortcoming, we don't take it very seriously in terms of repentance.

A study of the Hebrew and Greek words that are translated "patient" or "patience" reveals that in the original languages their meanings are far from superficial. The King James Version most often translates these words as "longsuffering." Suffering is bad, but for an extended time it is really bad and hard to endure—emphasis on the "long" part. Every virtue requires practice if we want to become holy.

> It is only if we learn grace and wisdom in the face of smaller daily disappointments that we will be ready for the great ones.
> —Timothy Keller

My oldest son, Greg, lost an executive position in a job he loved. The company did a "reorg," and his role was eliminated. It was a big loss for him, and a few weeks afterward I asked him what he was learning. He replied, "Patience and trust." Trusting that God has your life in his hands makes patience more achievable. And knowing that hardships hold valuable lessons offers hopeful purpose in the suffering.

I especially appreciate the example of those people who can put life into perspective and face disappointment calmly and joyfully. Jeff Chacon's bride-to-be, Lisa, was staying with us before the big day. Her mom called me a few days before the wedding to say that the wrong wedding band had arrived at the jewelers. It was not the one that Lisa had ordered for Jeff. Her mom described it as "ugly." The apologetic jeweler said Lisa could use the ugly ring for the ceremony and trade it for the right ring after the honeymoon. Lisa's mom said she didn't want to tell Lisa about this terrible mistake; she wanted me to tell Lisa. I didn't argue about who should tell Lisa, but it was a conversation I immediately dreaded. When Lisa got home from work that day, I sat her down and broke the bad news. She smiled and shrugged and said, "Well, I'll still be married to Jeff!" Lisa had a grateful perspective that would not let any circumstance cloud her joy.

A no-matter-what kind of patience is such a blessing! No matter what, I am going to heaven! That is the assurance that makes any trial possible to endure. How else could we consider trials a joy? (James 1:2). It does not mean we'll never grieve. Even Jesus wept. It does mean that we'll strive for a righteous response to every negative event in our lives.

The Apostle Paul understood suffering and he understood patience. He saw purpose in both, and he knew we are encouraged by each other's examples. He offered his own example to the Corinthians: "If we are distressed, it is for your comfort and salvation; if we are comforted, it is for your comfort, which produces in you patient endurance of the same sufferings we suffer" (II Corinthians 1:6). Hebrews 6:12 confirms the need for examples: "Imitate those who through faith and patience inherit what has been promised."

Sometimes we hide our pain, thinking it will discourage others, when in fact, it makes us more relatable and often is the example people need. It is hard if we think we'll receive platitudes or unwanted admonitions instead of empathy. But we need to take the risk in the hope that our vulnerability will be just what someone else needs to see.

I have a terrible time being patient with injustice. I want fairness at all times, in all situations. (This is not the place where I am going to admit how unfair *I* can be!) I want everyone to obey traffic laws. I don't like people to cut in line. I don't want anyone to cheat at a game I'm playing with them.

I was recently waiting for a parking space to be vacated. The car in the space I wanted had its back-up lights on, and I was sitting patiently with my turn signal on, indicating my intention to move into the space. Unfortunately, as soon as the car backed out, another car coming from the other direction whipped into the space before I could get my foot off the brake. No more patience for me! I was enraged at the injustice of this. I instantly attributed rudeness, meanness, and unconscionable disregard of the rights of others (me). I hate to admit it, but I gave my horn a long angry blast before moving on to find another parking place. Later, calmer reflection made me honestly ashamed, and I hope it served as a lesson for my heart to become more patient.

That was impatience at such a petty level. It surely could not be considered *long*suffering! God is looking for *holy* patience. He wants our patience to set us apart. Lots of people would find my outrage understandable. That's the thing—what grabs people's attention is our holiness, not our common sins. And while I want God to be able to use me as an example of holiness, mostly, I want to be like him because I love him. I want to be like him because I want him to be pleased with the growth of me, his daughter.

God is patient. It is soothing for me to remember this, but his patience is not designed to make me complacent about changing. To his glory, his patience gives me time to repent and grow.

What if God...bore with great patience the objects of his

wrath... What if he did this to make the riches of his glory known to the objects of his mercy, whom he prepared in advance for glory—even us? (Romans 9:22-24)

Jesus set the supreme example of patience. He was patient with the doubt of Thomas and the dullness of the disciples he was trying to teach. He was patient with the weak faith of Peter and the insensitivity of the three who fell asleep when he had asked them to pray in Gethsemane. He was patient with injustice at a level that only martyrs will experience. I am personally stunned by his silence and humility in the face of outrageously fabricated accusations and an agonizing death. His was a patience born of love, as demonstrated by his plea on the cross for God to forgive the torturers who put him there. I've got such a long way to go! I blared my horn in a parking lot. (Hopefully, no more.)

The book of Revelation was written primarily to offer hope and courage to Christians facing torment and martyrdom. "This calls for patient endurance on the part of the people of God who keep his commands and remain faithful to Jesus" (Revelation 14:12). Patience defined: remaining faithfully righteous no matter what, no matter how long, to the end.

God is unequivocally righteous, so it's a no-brainer to conclude that he is patient. Evidence of his patience is the fact that he has not annihilated humanity even though we sin and sin and sin. He got fed up with us once and sent a flood, but even then he waited 100 years before the deluge, offering people the chance to change (I Peter 3:20). And then he let every future generation try again with a plan in place to forgive us through the death of his Son.

It is easy to take God's patience for granted because the earth is still spinning. That's dangerous! We should take his patience personally. He loves us. He wants us to spend eternity with him. He's waiting for us to repent, but he won't wait forever. We will not escape God's judgment.

> *Or do you show contempt for the riches of his kindness, forbearance and patience, not realizing that God's kindness is intended to lead you to repentance?* (Romans 2:4)

Anyway, God is patient and he wants us to be patient. Sometimes we fake a calm composure or remain outwardly poised when we are upset just so we can feel better about ourselves or to play to the audience around us, the people we feel a need to please. But God wants the real thing. He wants to shape us into who he is. He wants us to ask for his help in learning patience. He wants us to ask each other for help. He wants us to look for the examples of patience around us. It is good to practice on the little stuff, because the big stuff may be right around the corner.

• Meditation •

Your statutes are my delight; they are my counselors.
— Psalm 119:24

Kindness can become its own motive. We are made
kind by being kind. —Eric Hoffer

Chapter 7

Holy Kindness

Kindness in America seems almost like an intermittent fad. I don't know any follow-up statistics on the "random acts of kindness" or "pay it forward" movements, but the interest appears to have waned. Hopping on board these feel-good activities offered interesting stories to share on Facebook and brief feelings of self-satisfaction. They were great ideas, and hopefully they were a springboard for some kind habits, but the outcome does not seem to be that we have become a nation of kinder people.

God has a different idea about kindness. What sets apart the kindness that God embodies and advocates is that it is a quality that grows within and is continuously exhibited without. He wants us to be kind, not just occasionally but always, as the outpouring of a compassionate heart. God hopes that when people think of Christians, they will think of kindness. This kindness is considerate, thoughtful, polite, warmhearted, helpful, benevolent, and courteous. Someone with this sort of kindness has developed an innate sensitivity to the needs of others.

Holy kindness is not mundane or bland. It is noteworthy; it is out of the norm. Think of the Good Samaritan, a parable Jesus shared, as recorded in Luke 10:25–37. A poor man was robbed and beaten and left for dead on the side of the road. A priest and a Levite in succession purposely avoided offering help. It was a Samaritan who took stock of this unfortunate victim's needs and fully met them on the spot. He not only got out his first-aid kit and ministered to the guy, but he put the guy on his own donkey to take him to long-term care. Delivering him to an inn, he paid the innkeeper to care for the man, and even promised to return and pay any other expenses incurred in his absence. It is a challenging example of kindness—and that was exactly Jesus' point! No everyday, ordinary story of kindness would do to show this expert in the law his need to change his thoughts and behavior. The message for each of us is clear: do all that you can! We should never avoid the inconvenience of kindness. The grand opportunities may appear only occasionally, but the smaller ones are everywhere, all the time.

We can make hospital visits or take meals to shut-ins; we can shovel the snow from a neighbor's walkway; we can write encouraging notes or go to a friend's home to pray with them when they have suffered a tragedy; we can smile at strangers or let a weary shopper with a single item go ahead of us in a grocery line. We can sign up for more structured opportunities, like mission trips to volunteer in orphanages or build houses for the homeless, or to serve closer to home in a soup kitchen. We can initiate kind conversations and show genuine interest in someone who seems unrelatable to us. Maybe we can bridge age and cultural differences just by being curious and caring. I'm not trying to offer an exhaustive list, but these are examples of opportunities that are all around us and don't even require the effort of a difficult search (or the bank account the Samaritan must have had; but if we've got it, God thinks we ought to use it generously to show kindness).

Kindness is born of love. There may be no payback, no "karma" that ensures a boomerang of lovingkindness. But there's a great incentive in knowing that God notices and smiles, and that is the greatest reward we could ever hope for!

> *But love your enemies, do good to them, and lend to them without expecting to get anything back. Then your reward will be great, and you will be children of the Most High, because he is kind to the ungrateful and wicked. Be merciful, just as your Father is merciful.* (Luke 6:35-36)

Kindness is deeply rooted in compassion. The ability to feel for (be compassionate with) someone else who is in need and seek to meet that need (be kind), makes us more like God. Compassion is one of the first ways God wanted Moses to introduce him to the Israelites.

> *"The LORD, the LORD, the compassionate and gracious God, slow to anger, abounding in love and faithfulness, maintaining love to thousands, and forgiving wickedness, rebellion and sin. Yet he does not leave the guilty unpunished."* (Exodus 34:6-7)

David wrote about the compassion of God (Psalm 86:5, 103:13, 116:5, 145:8–9). Even Jeremiah, while lamenting the fate of Judah when God punished them for their blatant idolatry, praised God for his compassion (Lamentations 3:22).

Okay, here's a thought about the compassion of God—it doesn't even qualify as a theory; it's just a thought. Sometimes when I suggest something to my husband, he jokingly says, "That's a thought. It's not a good thought, but it's a thought." Maybe that comment fits here? Anyway, you know how people ask (maybe you ask) why God would create people when they hurt him by sinning and some of them end up going to hell. I don't know. It's really none of our business. He owes us no explanation, but even if he gave one, we probably wouldn't get it.

Some say that it is because he needed someone to love. That does not make sense to me because he had the Son and the Spirit and all the angels to love. Others speculate that it is necessary in the great cosmic battle between God and Satan. Maybe there had to be a contest with measurable results for good to win and evil to lose. Interesting, and still, none of our business.

Here is my vaporous thought: we give God an outlet for compassion. Compassion is that aspect of love that has care and concern for someone's needs. In heaven, the Son and Spirit have no needs. Jesus had to come to earth to experience being needy— physically, emotionally, and spiritually. We are all needy people.

There's a tenderness about compassion. Compassion steps outside self-interest and into the emotional, physical, and spiritual needs of others. However, needs can be met physically without compassion, like the irritated server who grudgingly brings your meal. She met your need, but without any heart investment. She probably has something going on that cries out about her own need for compassion.

It is hard to be kind to the unkind. Jesus did it every day while he walked the earth. It is surprising to note that of the thousands he taught, fed, and healed, only 120 were faithful to him after his death (Acts 1:15). The unkind may repay kindness with indifference or insult. It happened to Jesus. He wasn't blind to the unkind ways people responded to him. He took note of the lepers who failed to thank him for their healing (Luke 17:11–19). He pointed out the hypocrisy of the Pharisee who invited him for dinner but failed to show him the common courtesy of a host (Luke 7:36–50).

Compassion is feeling for someone. Several Hebrew and

Greek words end up in English translations as "compassion." They variously mean "having mercy," "to have yearning bowels," "to love," "to show kindness," or "to pity."

God's kindness and compassion are not sappy and sentimental. They are holy and, as such, inseparable from truth. It is said that a true friend will tell you if you have spinach in your teeth. God is like that. He does not, in a fake display of kindness, overlook sin. He exposes it. He forgives, but he keeps his promise that we will reap what we sow. It would be unkind if he had not warned us, but he has—through his word, through the recorded example of his Son, and through the courageous, and hopefully gentle, prodding of disciples.

Since compassion is embedded in God's nature, perhaps that is why Jesus didn't just appear on earth as an adult and die for us the next day. Jesus spent thirty-three years down here. He didn't just want to feel *for* us, he wanted to feel *with* us. The incarnation of Jesus enabled God to say, "I get it! I've experienced that too." The Greek word *sumpatheo* can be literally translated "to feel with." This word is found only once in the Bible, in Hebrews 4:15 referring to the role of high priest that Jesus now plays in our lives.

> *For we do not have a high priest who is unable to empathize [sumpatheo] with our weaknesses, but we have one who has been tempted in every way, just as we are—yet he did not sin. Let us then approach God's throne of grace with confidence, so that we may receive mercy and find grace to help us in our time of need. (Hebrews 4:15-16)*

This is stunning to me! Jesus didn't just die for us; he didn't live only to select twelve followers who could carry on his mission; he lived so he could experience the same struggles we do. It was the only time in eternity when God made himself vulnerable to Satan, and he was victorious! Every day he spent on earth, he experienced circumstances that many of us would consider disappointing and annoying, and he met them with compassion. He now stands at the right hand of God interceding on our behalf (Romans 8:34). Jesus pleads our case to his Father with empathy. Since God went to great lengths to have empathy for us, we should never doubt it or take it for granted.

Empathy for one another ought to come naturally, even automatically. We have all known joy and sorrow, comfort and pain. We have all experienced sin and regret. Still, instead of empathy, we become critical and judgmental. Unfortunately, looking down on our fellow humans can feed our egos, as though we were superior. So sad; so wrong.

Because Paul, through inspiration, listed the "fruits of the Spirit" as separate entities, we might mistakenly conclude that they each stand alone. No, they are inseparably linked—in a way, we can't have any one of them without the others. We have different strengths, and some of us are better at some fruits than others. Any strength we have will feed the development of the others. God wants them to flow from transformed hearts that mirror his heart. They're a package deal—because "love is kind."

God wants us to be kind to the poor (Proverbs 19:17), kind to each other (Ephesians 4:32), and kind to our enemies (Romans 12:20). He even wants us to speak kindly (Colossians 4:6). Real kindness is holy. And because we belong to God, it is not just something we do, it's who we are to become.

> *Therefore, as God's chosen people, holy and dearly loved, clothe yourselves with compassion, kindness, humility, gentleness, and patience. (Colossians 3:12)*

• Meditation •

But when the kindness and love of God our Savior
appeared, he saved us, not because of righteous things we had
done, but because of his mercy.
— Titus 3:4-5

> Goodness is...the character of the Deity; and without it, man is a busy, mischievous, wretched thing. —Sir Francis Bacon

Chapter 8

Holy Goodness

Righteousness, virtue, benevolence, generosity... Translators have used each of these words as synonyms for goodness—different version, different word, but the meaning is consistent (the Greek word is *agathosune*). God is the very definition of goodness.

The word "good" appears in many places throughout the Bible, but the word "goodness" appears only a handful of times. It is the word in Galatians 5:22–23 that reveals that goodness is a fruit of God's Spirit. We have been called "by his own glory and goodness" to emulate him (II Peter 1:3). We recognize that it is a special honor for God to want us to be like him; yet we also know it's a high calling and the effort of a lifetime.

I don't think the order of those fruits has significance, although we might suspect that it does, since love is listed first. Also, other scriptures teach us that love holds preeminence and that other noble qualities are irrelevant and perhaps nonexistent without love as a foundation. Conversely, love falls last on the list of virtues found in II Peter 1:5–7. Some might say that is because you have to work up to it. My friend Debbie once said, "I think we've achieved brotherly kindness (the characteristic right before love in the NASB), and we think it's love, but I think when we get to love it will blow our minds!" I have always thought she was onto something. But while these verses encourage us to "make every effort" to grow in these virtues, I somehow doubt they are in consecutive order. All of us have different strengths and weaknesses. While some excel in a specific trait and provide a helpful example to the rest of us, we will most likely find ourselves needing to work on several at once. The operative word here is "work"—that's the "every effort" part.

If we are working at goodness, what would that look like? It would look like tenderness, benevolence, altruism, harmlessness, humility. It would look like taking soup to a sick neighbor or standing up for someone who is being mistreated. It would look like lots of things we are familiar with. Psalm 34:14 tells us to "turn from evil and do good." Goodness is visible in the doing.

Good deeds certainly spring from goodness in the heart: integrity, honesty, thoughtfulness. We are created in the image of God (Genesis 1:26). Because God is the Creator, we are gifted with creativity. Creative goodness within us has enabled even unbelievers to do inspiring good. Nonprofits have been formed by agnostics seeking to serve the needy and disadvantaged. That is all because of God, whether they give him the credit or not.

A trap we can fall into is thinking we are the source of our goodness. While our egos are soothed and inflated by this, we are telling ourselves a feel-good lie. We mustn't kid ourselves. Any wisdom, righteousness, or holiness does not emanate from our own goodness and savvy. God puts good impulses in our hearts and provides the opportunities that come along and the skill or strength that we possess (Ephesians 2:10). He alone gets the credit for any good we do. That knowledge will keep us from playing silent one-upmanship when we are tempted to compare ourselves to others and feel superior in the good-deed department.

We do not dare to classify or compare ourselves with some who commend themselves. When they measure themselves by themselves and compare themselves with themselves, they are not wise. (II Corinthians 10:12)

Paul wrote to the Corinthian church, "You are in Christ Jesus, who has become for us wisdom from God—that is, our righteousness, holiness and redemption" (I Corinthians 1:30). I love this! These things that Jesus' life and death have purchased for me are treasures. I bask in this knowledge and base my hope on it. I have to remind myself of this continually because I am so prone to focus on my own inadequacy instead of his all-sufficiency. The eternal goodness of Jesus was demonstrated during his life on earth and gave us a well-defined picture of the goodness of God.

To offload my own awareness of my guilt, it's tempting to mentally eliminate any onus on me to try to be good and just leave it all up to Jesus. He is certainly up to the task, but it's not how God designed it. How could we be a light to the world or a city on a hill (Matthew 5:14–16) if we just sat around content with our own imperfection? It's another trap Satan tries to use. He wants us to be complacent about our personal responsibility to pursue goodness.

Jesus knows living on earth makes it hard to be good (Hebrews 4:15). This is why Peter instructs us to "make every effort." And effort it will take. In my experience, the longer you make the effort, the more effort it takes. I think this is because as time goes on, superficial ungodly traits in our characters have been pretty much confessed and addressed. It is those deep, ingrained, and often unnoticed character sins that lurk behind. Because God longs for us to "participate in [his] divine nature" (II Peter 1:4) so we can resemble him and shine in a lost world, he calls us to try hard:

> *For this very reason, make every effort to add to your faith goodness; and to goodness, knowledge; and to knowledge, self-control; and to self-control, perseverance; and to perseverance, godliness; and to godliness, mutual affection; and to mutual affection, love. For if you possess these qualities in increasing measure, they will keep you from being ineffective and unproductive in your knowledge of our Lord Jesus Christ. But whoever does not have them is nearsighted and blind, forgetting that they have been cleansed from their past sins. (II Peter 1:5-9)*

With perfect goodness Jesus taught, comforted, healed, and raised people from the dead. He was good to the ungrateful (Luke 17:11–19). He is even good to evil people (Matthew 5:45).

Pursuing goodness is an exploration of faith. Paul counseled the Ephesian church to "live as children of light (for the fruit of the light consists in all goodness, righteousness and truth) and find out what pleases the Lord" (Ephesians 5:8–10). Being a light in a dark world and learning increasingly how to please God—that's goodness and that's the grand adventure!

I am very encouraged by II Thessalonians 1:11: "We constantly pray for you, that our God may make you worthy of his calling, and that by his power he may bring to fruition your every desire for goodness and your every deed prompted by faith." The reason this verse means so much to me is that I'm painfully aware that I am not worthy (aka, deserving) of God's calling. It is by his power, not my own, that my desire for goodness can be realized. I don't have the power to be worthy—too late for that! I used to gasp in shame every time I read Ephesians 4:1 and feel both hopeless and helpless in the face of Paul's call to "live a life worthy of the calling you have received." I had the same defeated response to other verses in

Scripture calling me to worthiness (I Thessalonians 2:12; Philippians 1:27; Colossians 1:10). Taken together with II Thessalonians 1:11, they all make sense to me. I can trust God for my worthiness! He will supply my goodness, "for it is God who works in you to will and to act in order to fulfill his good purpose." Philippians 2:13). I once heard someone say that God's mercy fills in the gap between our goodness and the perfection that makes us worthy.

What a good God! He supplies both the impulse and the opportunities for goodness and the results of the efforts we exert. And then he fills in the gaps. He wants us to be successful at goodness. He wants to make us holy. It frees us up to try; it empowers us to make every effort!

• Meditation •

I will consider all your works and meditate on all your mighty deeds.
— Psalm 77:12

Let us have faith...and in that faith, let us, to the end, dare to do our duty.
—Abraham Lincoln

Chapter 9

Holy Faithfulness

The sure dependability of God's faithfulness is a resounding theme throughout the Bible. It's what makes us able to take the Bible seriously. We can take him at his word. We can count on his promises.

In his dealings with the Israelite nation, God proved himself to be faithful without exception. The Old Testament is a remarkable treatise on his faithfulness covering a lengthy history with Israel (more than two thousand years), and it is to our benefit to study it, believe it, and trust it.

> *Know therefore that the LORD your God is God; he is the faithful God, keeping his covenant of love to a thousand generations of those who love him and keep his commandments. (Deuteronomy 7:9)*

God's statutes for us are a "covenant of love." How could they be anything else? After all, he *is* love! He didn't one day sit around heaven and think up rules to restrict our pleasure and become our dictator. In love, he gave us precepts that are for our highest good, and he gave us the freedom to obey them or not. If God were capricious or impulsive, he would deserve to be disregarded. If he changed his mind about what is right and what is wrong, or if he reworked his laws to fit cultural differences and time periods, we should look for another God. If he liked us one day and hated us the next; if he promised goodness and delivered evil; if he were easily distracted by whimsy, and thus, often unavailable to us, he would be a prime source of well-founded insecurity.

As with every aspect of God's character, his faithfulness is stable, irrefutable, and eternal (Psalm 117:2). It is impossible for him not to be faithful. Unlike us who are up and down in our faithfulness to God, to others and to ourselves, God's own nature prohibits him from instability. Looking back on myself as a mother, I am so ashamed that my children sometimes had to assess what mood I was in to approach me. Not so with God. We can come to him with full assurance that he has no shadows clouding his reception of us (James 1:17). Faithfulness is who he is.

> If we are faithless,
>   he remains faithful,
>   for he cannot disown himself. (II Timothy 2:13)

Every word from him is trustworthy. He is faithful to his word. That is good news for those of us who are believers of his word; it is bad news for those who have chosen to live otherwise. His faithfulness is just. Whoever we are, however we live, good or bad, zealous or lukewarm, he has the same standard for all of us.

> The Lord, the Lord, the compassionate and gracious God, slow to anger, abounding in love and faithfulness, maintaining love to thousands, and forgiving wickedness, rebellion and sin. Yet he does not leave the guilty unpunished. (Exodus 34:6)

> *He is the Rock, his works are perfect,*
>   *and all his ways are just.*
> *A faithful God who does no wrong,*
>   *upright and just is he.* (Deuteronomy 32:4)

Praise for the faithfulness of God is a recurring theme throughout the book of Psalms (Psalm 33:4; 36:5; 40:11; 57:10; 71:22; 86:15; 89:1, 8, 14; 100:5; 108:4; 111:7; 145:13). Those are just a few! These verses are worth study and meditation. His faithfulness is a blessing we should never regard lightly. His dependability should evoke both gratitude and fear. But primarily it should evoke praise. He is a God we can count on! His faithfulness should leave us awestruck. It is unequaled in any other being apart from God the Father, God the Son, and God the Holy Spirit.

> *LORD, you are my God;*
>   *I will exalt you and praise your name,*
> *for in perfect faithfulness*
>   *you have done wonderful things,*
>   *things planned long ago.* (Isaiah 25:1)

Naturally, Immanuel ("God with us") bore exactly the same qualities of faithfulness. Jesus was faithful to his Father and faithful to us. He was unashamed to announce to his enemies, "The one who sent me is with me; he has not left me alone, for I always do what pleases him" (John 8:29). There are many examples of Jesus' faithfulness to God, but most impacting is his example of submission (faithfulness) to the will of God the night before his death. Struggling with the horror of the death he was facing, he nevertheless prayed, "My Father, if it is possible, may this cup be taken from me. Yet not as I will, but as you will" (Matthew 26:39).

He was faithful to his Father's will and faithful to our hope for salvation.

And he was victorious! Faithfulness to God requires going into battle. There is a war going on every day, and our souls are the objects of conquest. Being faithful is painful, but it is worth the battle scars. Because God is faithful to provide a way for our salvation, Jesus rose from the dead as the "first fruits" of resurrection. The vision of this victorious King is most captivating in Revelation 19:11 and 13: "I saw heaven standing open and there before me was a white horse, whose rider is called faithful and true... He is dressed in a robe dipped in blood, and his name is the Word of God."

Back from battle, this is our Lord! He is forever King! He conquered death, and he offers us life if we will be faithful.

When I look at the fruits of his spirit—love, joy, peace, patience, kindness, goodness, faithfulness, gentleness, self-control—I find I have failed in every area. I need a conquering King because I am a battle-weary soldier and too weak for the fight. Still, those combined fruits are the standard I look to when I am searching for my true north. When I am whirling with anxiety, suffering grief, attacked by fear, or raging with anger, I measure myself by the nature of God and see where I need to grow. My progress on the road to perfection falls far short of the gains I would like to make, but without keeping the goal in sight, I would make little to no progress at all.

It is a humbling exercise to use the fruits of the Spirit as a plumb line, and I think that is what God intended. Are we faithful to God in every area of our lives? Do we faithfully love our enemies? Are we faithful to our marriage vows to love and respect? Are we faithfully patient with our children? Are we faithful to help the poor? Are we faithful to our friends? Are we faithfully devoted to the Christ's church? You get the idea. I don't know what fruit God is hoping you will grow in today, but he is always working on one or another primarily, and all of them always. He wants our characters to bear a family resemblance to his. He wants us to be faithful.

I do want to be faithful to God. I am not as far along as I expected to be in my eighth decade, and it is my nature to feel discouraged by that, but it's about progress. Looking back, I can see growth and it gives me hope.

• Meditation •

Your love, Lord, reaches to the heavens, your faithfulness to the skies.
— Psalm 36:5

It is a fool who mistakes gentleness for weakness.
—Anonymous

Chapter 10

Holy Gentleness

My friend Susan's second son was less than a year old when he became miserably ill. He was inconsolable night and day for several consecutive nights. It was not a life-threatening illness, but Scotty needed the comforting attention of a mom 24/7. Sleep deprived and weary, Susan told me she prayed for God to please send an angel to hold Scotty so she could get some rest. She said that's when God told her, "You are the angel I have sent." Susan summoned the strength she didn't know she had to find the gentle care Scotty needed until he got well and returned to a normal, healthy sleep routine.

There are myriad accounts of moms who found courage and sometimes superhuman strength to meet their children's needs in times of crises. It explains why the Apostle Paul used the example of a mother's gentleness to remind the Thessalonians of how he treated them when he was with them (I Thessalonians 2:7–8).

Because of God's power and unwavering standards, some think of him as being harsh. Not so. A God who would let his Son die for us is a God of love and strong gentleness.

Elijah learned about the gentleness of God in a dramatic experience. When Jezebel sought to murder him following his bold and humiliating defeat of the prophets of the idol Baal, Elijah's courage waned. After such an amazing victory (I Kings 18), it is hard to imagine that he would run in fear and cower in a cave, but that is what he did. Since God had used Elijah so mightily and displayed such enormous power, it might even have seemed reasonable for God to rebuke him for panicking: "How can you be such a faithless wimp after the miracles you have just witnessed?" But that is not what God did, and I am so glad! We need to know this gentle side of God—and God thought Elijah did, too!

> *And the word of the LORD came to him: "What are you doing here, Elijah?"*
>
> *He replied, "I have been very zealous for the LORD God Almighty. The Israelites have rejected your covenant, torn down your altars, and put your prophets to death with the sword. I am the only one left, and now they are trying to kill me too."*
>
> *The LORD said, "Go out and stand on the mountain in the presence of the LORD, for the LORD is about to pass by."*
>
> *Then a great and powerful wind tore the mountains apart and shattered the rocks before the LORD, but the LORD was not in the wind. After the wind there was an earthquake, but the LORD was not in the earthquake. After the earthquake came a fire, but the LORD was not in the fire. And after the fire came a gentle whisper. When Elijah heard it, he pulled his cloak over his face and went out and stood at the mouth of the cave. (I Kings 19:9-13)*

There was no less strength in the whisper than in the gale force wind, the earthquake, or the fire, but it was the reassuring side of God that Elijah needed at that time. That whisper assured him of God's tenderness, compassion, and approachability. God still planned to continue using Elijah, and he still expected Elijah to be obedient, because God's gentleness is a strong gentleness.

Jesus wanted us to know his gentleness too: "Come to me, all you who are weary and burdened, and I will give you rest. Take my yoke upon you and learn from me, for I am gentle and humble in heart, and you will find rest for your souls." What a precious invitation to come to a gentle and humble Savior! What a magnificent promise—rest for our souls! There is still a yoke and an entreaty to learn. It is that same strong gentleness that Elijah experienced.

These are important examples because the Greek word for gentle (*prautes*) has no English equivalent. It combines too many concepts to cram into a one-word translation. Here are the concepts that combine to more accurately understand the original Greek: the power to soothe or calm, forgiving, polite, humble, courteous, understanding, equanimity, able to remain courteous and strong without rage or abuse, a calmness that breeds confidence, strength plus gentleness.

Paul told Timothy to look for this quality of gentleness in a man he would seek to appoint as an elder in God's church (I Timothy 3:3). But he called Timothy to first aspire to this characteristic himself when he instructed him to "pursue righteousness, godliness, faith, love, endurance, and gentleness. Fight the good fight of the faith" (I Timothy 6:11–12). Both the tenderness and the fight harmonize in the Christian character. It takes uncommon strength to be gentle.

The book of James includes gentleness in the list of qualities that make up godly wisdom. It is not the way the world defines wisdom, but the world almost always recognizes someone bearing this wisdom as having a superior demeanor.

But the wisdom that is from above is first of all pure, then peaceable, gentle, and easy to be intreated, full of mercy and good fruits, without partiality, and without hypocrisy. (James 3:17 KJV)

But the wisdom that comes from heaven is first of all pure; then peace-loving, considerate, submissive, full of mercy and good fruit, impartial and sincere. (James 3:17 NIV)

A comparison of these translations of James 3:17—and, perhaps, a compilation—gives a fuller picture of the original intent of the Holy Spirit and a richer meaning to the gentleness God is expecting of us. It is a high and holy calling; it is a set-apart gentleness. It takes some serious meditation for me to measure my thoughts and actions against this expanded English definition of gentleness. Maybe you will find that to be true for yourself also.

In revealing the qualities of character God prizes in a Christian woman, Peter wrote of "the unfading beauty of a gentle and quiet spirit" (I Peter 3:4–6). It is good to know he wasn't talking about a docile, weak-willed woman, but one with the strength to be calm and secure in the Lord. She can submit to her husband's needs without the frailty that might give way to the possibly unreasonable or ungodly wants of an unbelieving man. She is no doormat, but a strong and equal partner who is thoughtful, kind, and cooperative. And that is what God calls husbands and singles, young and old to be as well:

Be completely humble and gentle; be patient, bearing with one another in love. (Ephesians 4:2)

Therefore, as God's chosen people, holy and dearly loved, clothe yourselves with compassion, kindness, humility, gentleness and patience. (Colossians 3:12)

77

We are called to a kind of gentleness that has backbone. It has the strength to be steadfast and courteous, to hold to deep convictions without rancor. It can sooth and calm, and it is neither weak nor quarrelsome. It is never hysterical. And it is not optional. God repeats the exhortation to Christians again and again. We should stay on our knees asking God to fill us with his kind of gentleness. It emits a glow that lights up the darkness.

• Meditation •

Let your gentleness be evident to all. The Lord is near.
— Philippians 4:5

If you would learn self-mastery, begin by yielding yourself
to the One Great Master. —Johann Friedrich Lobstein

Chapter 11

Holy Self-Control

I guess resisting any temptation requires self-control. Wouldn't it have been great if Eve had summoned the self-control to turn away from that forbidden fruit! Somehow, still, I associate self-control with food, yet it is not just an act of self-denial; like the other fruits of the Spirit, it is a character strength. We don't always associate kindness and goodness with strength, but as with a deeper understanding of gentleness, we come to understand that every aspect of God's character is strong. But we already knew that self-control requires strength.

Self-control is the one fruit that seems to lack the beatific qualities of the others. Picture the facial expressions we associate with love, joy, peace, and so forth; then in contrast, picture the countenance of self-control—gritted teeth, pinched and pained. It is easy to see the benefits of the rest of the fruits as they extend themselves to bless others. But self-control...well, it's all about self. I guess it helps others when we restrain ourselves from lashing out at them in a moment of rage, but often we are the sole benefactors of controlling ourselves. Still, instead of feeling blessed by self-control, we tend to feel deprived. It seems we only think of self-control in terms of rigid self-denial. We feel like the victims of a blessing!

Self-control sometimes results in self-pity. Shame on us! That may be the difference between winners and losers. Winners celebrate self-control; losers wallow in self-pitying sorrow over deprivation.

When Lissa's husband left her and their children for another woman, her lawyer urged her to sue for alimony. Alimony would have been a fair condition of the divorce. On one level, Lissa was tempted, simply because of need, but she refused to ask for any money. There is nothing wrong with applying for alimony, but Lissa felt that at that early point in her shock, anger, and grief, suing for alimony would have felt vengeful, and she refused to consider a plea for money until she was sure she had completely forgiven him. Through daily effort and faithful prayer, she worked with God to cleanse her heart and be sure she was free of any desire for revenge. Years later, her heart is free, and she and her children have lived very modestly while watching her ex-husband and his new wife become wealthy. Lissa has never asked for or received a penny. Forgiveness often requires self-denial, and self-denial usually requires self-control.

Naturally, the greatest example of God's self-control is found at the cross. Jesus controlled a desire to avoid the pain of torture and separation from his Father. God controlled a father's desire to protect his child. The agony of God's restraint found expression as "darkness came over all the land... The earth shook, the rocks split, and the tombs broke open"—the tortured heart of a father (Matthew 27:45, 51–52).

The righteousness and justice of God certainly sometimes pulled him toward annihilating his creation, but his mercy and self-control won out again and again. For instance, he could have immediately sent a flood to destroy the world when "every inclination of the thoughts of the human heart was only evil all the time" (Genesis 6:5); he could have miraculously instituted another plan.

Instead, he waited while Noah built an ark and pleaded with people to repent. Waiting requires self-control.

> *...to those who were disobedient long ago when God waited patiently in the days of Noah while the ark was being built. (I Peter 3:20)*

There is a demeanor of calm strength, a boldness in silence, a clinging to approachability and reasonableness in the face of hysteria and injustice. Repeatedly the Bible calls believers to this deportment. It should never be mistaken for passivity. When Judas came to kiss him in greedy betrayal, Jesus simply said, "Do what you came for, friend" (Matthew 26:50). Self-control? Yes— I can think of lots of things I would have been tempted to call Judas besides friend. As Jesus stood before the Sanhedrin and listened to the lying accusations from false witnesses, he remained silent (Matthew 26:59–63). Self-control? Absolutely!

Every awesome attribute of God's nature—even his anger and judgment—always exists in the context of his love, righteousness, self-control, and compassion. We need to ask ourselves what motivates our self-control. Hermas called self-restraint the "daughter of faith." Our faith certainly should motivate us to have self-control, but sometimes it is off our radar, or requires more effort than we are willing to invest. We are called to the same self-control God embodies—a holy self-control. We will never reach the same perfection of God's self-control, but it is the goal, and if we are aiming in the right direction, we'll get closer and closer over time.

I have thanked God many times for his merciful self-restraint. I know that if God were given to impulse—even uncontrolled righteous anger—he would have flicked me off the face of the earth by now. I still live and breathe because of the compassionate self-control of God.

> Because of the LORD's great love we are not consumed,
>   for his compassions never fail.
> They are new every morning;
>   great is your faithfulness. (Lamentations 3:22-23)

Surely if you have ever read through the Old Testament, you have been struck by the repeated faithlessness of the Israelite nation. From their insulting fear and complaining even after being miraculously delivered from Egyptian bondage, to their repeated egregious idolatry, God kept rescuing them. When they broke their end of the bargain, God kept his, although most of us would say that failure on their side gave the right to the other party to be released from the contract. But God keeps his promises no matter what and no matter the self-control it takes.

> They remembered that God was their Rock,
>   that God Most High was their Redeemer.
> But then they would flatter him with their mouths,
>   lying to him with their tongues;
> their hearts were not loyal to him,
>   they were not faithful to his covenant.
> Yet he was merciful;
>   he forgave their iniquities
>   and did not destroy them.
> Time after time he restrained his anger
>   and did not stir up his full wrath. (Psalm 78:35-38)

Translators have used various English words to capture the

meaning of the Greek word for self-control, *egkrateia*. These include temperance, self-restraint, and continence. But scholars today agree that the best translation is "self-control," which most fully communicates to English speakers the original intent of Scripture. The meaning is rich and reaches every aspect of the moral values we are offered, because every fruit of the Spirit requires self-control to obtain.

> It is *egkrateia* that makes love chastity and not lust.
> —William Barkley

This control starts in the heart and mind. Paul told the Corinthians that as Christians "we take captive every thought to make it obedient to Christ" (II Corinthians 10:5). What a high calling! It is definitely a set-apart way of thinking. As an antidote to anxiety, he said this: "Finally, brothers and sisters, whatever is true, whatever is noble, whatever is right, whatever is pure, whatever is lovely, whatever is admirable—if anything is excellent or praiseworthy—think about such things" (Philippians 4:8). I think it is an antidote to a lot more than anxiety. It counteracts every negative mindset. But it is not easy—believe me, I try! I long for the delightful purity of this kind of thinking.

Too often, we try to control our behavior without starting with our hearts and minds. Self-control is hypocrisy when we only restrain our baser natures to present a righteous appearance. While we are working on being like Christ, we may find that our hearts have to catch up with our actions. This is not hypocrisy. If we control our behavior without controlling our hearts, it is not a wasted moral exercise if we are making every effort to grow within. But this external control often finds us out of touch with our hearts and lulls us into complacency, thinking we have arrived. It is not healthy to "naval gaze," and that is not what I'm advocating. But we are at war. We are not just fighting for doctrinal purity or radical evangelism or some other worthy goal, we are fighting a personal battle to be like Jesus. Self-control is submitting to our values. We have got to be honest with ourselves and with God. We must humbly confess to a trusted friend when our hearts don't match our behavior and ask for prayers (James 5:16). In our battle between body and spirit, our prayers must appeal to the only source of power who can change our hearts.

Most of us prize self-control, but it can be foolishly and sinfully pursued and misdefined. I am thinking of life-threatening hazing in college fraternities (once common) or the dangerous or deforming rites that conferred manhood on boys in primitive societies. They required self-control, for sure, but accomplished nothing to purify righteousness in hearts. The dangerous game of Chicken may be a valid example.

More than thirty years ago our local news was alive with reports of a fatal hit-and-run only blocks away from our house. It was horrifying to pass by the white outline of a young boy's body after he had been hit by a car in the early morning hours.

Obviously, the police were investigating. They had a chip of paint and quickly traced it to a specific model car. That same day a woman from the neighborhood turned herself in. On her way to work she knew she had hit something, but she thought it was a bag of trash. It was predawn and very foggy on a hilly, two-lane road.

A young boy came forward to admit that he and his friend, now dead, had been playing a game of Chicken. They lay together in the road before dawn and waited for an oncoming car. The one to roll out of the way first was the "chicken." The one to stay longest in harm's way was declared the brave, self-controlled winner. In this sad case, the winner lost his life. I imagine the parents of these boys had taught them differently. I think they knew better than to sneak out of their houses in the dark and play a deadly game. I wish they had used their self-control to be obedient when an adrenaline rush called. There is no glory in misusing self-control.

> *Like a city whose walls are broken through*
> *is a person who lacks self-control. (Proverbs 25:28)*

Our current culture is far more accustomed to instant gratification than to self-control. Fast food drive-throughs, diamond lanes on the highway, ATMs instead of teller lines, express lanes at the grocery store, Amazon Prime, Siri and Alexa on command—it's all about quick convenience, but it makes us feel entitled to immediate service. It feeds our impatience.

It is a deeply blessed child who is raised in a home where patience, humility, and obedience are taught. A child learns self-control by first experiencing imposed control. I'm not talking about arbitrary restrictions just for the sake of rules; I'm talking about fair boundaries, clearly explained and consistently enforced in an atmosphere of love. It builds a strength of character that will serve that child well his whole life.

Maybe that is not how you were raised, and learning self-control is harder for you. It is worth the effort, and your motive can be the best and highest in the world: to become more like Jesus.

> *But mark this: There will be terrible times I the last days.*
> *People will be lovers of money, boastful, proud, abusive, disobe-*
> *dient to their parents, ungrateful, unholy, without love, unforgiving,*
> *slanderous, without self-control, brutal, not lovers of the good,*
> *treacherous, rash, conceited, lovers of pleasure rather than lovers*
> *of God. (II Timothy 3:1-4)*

We will find ourselves surrounded by an out-of-control culture. It makes our efforts to change to be Christlike harder in many ways, but more distinctive. Our battle is personal. Every fruit of the Spirit requires self-control to achieve, but this effort sets us apart. It makes us holy, and holiness is our goal!

• Meditation •

The mind controlled by the flesh is death, but the mind controlled by the Spirit is life and peace.
— Romans 8:6

The measure of love is compassion; the measure of compassion is kindness.
–Anonymous

Chapter 12

Holy Compassion

Compassion is not specifically listed in Galatians 5, but it is certainly a fruit of God's Spirit and is closely related to one of the fruits listed there: love. We know intuitively that we would not consider an uncompassionate God to be a loving God. In fact, it could be said of love and compassion that you can't have one without the other. I suppose we could demonstrate some compassionate acts without feeling love, but that is a philosophical debate. A compassionate demeanor can even be communicated when one is helpless to act, so it's not just about acting, but compassion will prompt us to act if it is within our power. Compassion can be extended without self-sacrifice, but it most mirrors the compassion of God when action and sacrifice are coupled.

For instance, when Jesus heard about the martyrdom of his cousin, John, he tried to escape "by boat privately to a solitary place," but "hearing of this, the crowds followed him." He had tried to grieve for a time in solitude—such a normal reaction, and so relatable to us. But, true to his nature, "when Jesus landed and saw a large crowd, he had compassion on them and healed their sick" (Matthew 14:12–14). Jesus' compassion came from his love for every man, woman and child.

In the Parable of the Lost Son, Jesus shows the son rebelliously leaving home and insensitively taking along an early inheritance. Years later the young man returned, and seeing him at a distance, the father "was filled with compassion for him; he ran to his son, threw his arms around him and kissed him" (Luke 15:11–22). Then he reinstated him to full sonship. The passage does not speak of extravagant love—or of patience, generosity, forgiveness, grace, or mercy, but they are all abundantly in evidence, along with the compassion that had the father running toward his son. That is what the set-apart compassion of God is like.

Little wonder, if we are to resemble God, that he calls us to compassion in both our character and behavior. Although it might seem just and even righteous to deny compassion to someone who clearly does not deserve it, God is not like that. If our worthiness determined whether we might receive God's compassion, we would be hopeless.

Longing for salvation is understandable. Longing for the character of God should come naturally to Christians. After all, we are the ones to "hunger and thirst for righteousness," and who pursue the other characteristics Jesus spoke about in his first public sermon (Matthew 5:1–12). It is noteworthy that in contrast to the Ten Commandments, this initial call of Jesus to the new covenant began with character traits, not behaviors. The entire New Testament calls us to emulate God's nature. We should long for compassion—not just from others, but toward others.

I am intrigued by the role of Jesus as our high priest (Hebrews 4:14–15). The Bible says that as a human he experienced every hardship and temptation that we do. The New International Version says that this enables him to "empathize" with our weaknesses. That word "empathize" is interesting. It literally means "to feel with." Most other versions translate the original Greek word, sumpatheo, as "sympathize." It looks a lot like our word "sympathize," and many translations simply say Jesus is able to "sympathize with our weaknesses." The KJV says he is "touched with the feeling of our infirmities." I am comforted by that. Jesus doesn't just feel for us at a distance. He feels with us. He gets us! He became like us and he wants us to become like him.

> *Therefore, as God's chosen people, holy and dearly loved, clothe yourselves with compassion, kindness, humility, gentleness and patience... Forgive as the Lord forgave you. And over all these virtues put on love, which binds them all together in perfect unity. (Colossians 3:12, 14)*

These qualities set Christians apart from the mainstream population. As our societies become more and more chaotic and divided, Christians bearing the image of God are truly the light in the darkness.

• Meditation •

The Lord is gracious and righteous; our God is full of compassion.
— Psalm 116:5

Humility is the foundation of all the other virtues, hence, in the soul in which this virtue does not exist there cannot be any other virtue except in mere appearance. —St. Augustine

Chapter 13

Holy Humility

Humility is not a characteristic often attributed to God. The truth is, however, that from the beginning, God's humility is evident. He deigned to create humankind in his own image. Then he stooped to initiating a connection with Adam and Eve. He walked with them and talked with them as friends. He didn't pretend to be their equal; he had laws for them to follow because he wanted them to thrive in the world he gave them. He knew what was best for them, but his humility and love caused him to let them choose their own way. He was not controlling then and is not controlling today. He is neither a dictator nor a tyrant.

It may be hard for us to think of God as being humble because, in our view, he has no reason to be. That's how we think—that being humble has to be based on some demeaning flaw in us. Although we may not want to admit it, we can think of humility as a position of inferiority—as if some have reason to be proud and some have reason to be humble. Outside of reasons, we choose to be humble when we choose to be like Jesus.

By coming to earth God (Emmanuel) fully displayed his humility. Enthroned in heaven, he left glory behind. Conceived by an unwed mother, he was lowborn, with a barn for a birthplace, poor, physically unattractive, and unappreciated. He grew up as a carpenter's son among siblings who didn't understand that he was deity (Mark 3:20–21). He didn't hang out with the elite; his best friends were from society's lower rung—they were fishermen, tax-collectors, and prostitutes (Matthew 11:19). He accepted invitations into homes where he was an unpopular curiosity (Luke 7:36–49). He never owned a piece of property although he owned the entire universe.

He willingly submitted to an unjust and shameful death—that is humility beyond what we will ever experience. It is also a humility that evades our full comprehension. God, the Creator, turned himself over to his created beings, who with unbridled arrogance sneered at him, mocked him, and, with the full extent of the human capacity for cruelty, tortured him to death (Luke 23:35–36; Philippians 2:8).

The opposite of humility is arrogance, entitlement, considering oneself better than others, and looking to one's own interests above the interests of others (cf. Philippians 2:3–4). One way or another, it shows up in our speech, our demeanor, our behavior, our attitudes and often on our faces. But even if we wear a humble mask, God can see what is in our hearts. Humility is not about insecurity or low self-esteem or a lack of self-confidence. It is what makes us confidently able to serve others and reserve center stage for someone else. Humility give us the ability to not take ourselves too seriously and, when appropriate, to laugh at ourselves. True humility carries a happy frame of mind. Christians know we are saved, not superior.

*LORD, what are human beings that you care for them,
mere mortals that you think of them? (Psalm 144:3)*

No title or position makes one human being better or more worthy than another. We are prone to measure abilities and talents on scales of our own making. But in Romans 12:3–8, in a passage about the different gifts God grants to his people, we are warned, "Do not think of yourself more highly than you ought, but rather think of yourself with sober judgment." Humility is the key to an accurate and righteous self-concept.

It is in vain to gather virtues without humility; for the Spirit of God
delights to dwell in the hearts of the humble.
—Erasmus

Humility is the offspring of wisdom. Those considered wise by the world's standards have no need to appear humble. Wisdom and humility are usually thought of as two distinct qualities—not so! The Bible says there are two kinds of wisdom—a false, worldly wisdom and the real thing.

*Who is wise and understanding among you? Let them show
it by their good life, by deeds done in humility that comes from
wisdom. But if you harbor bitter envy and selfish ambition in
your hearts, do not boast about it or deny the truth. Such
"wisdom" does not come down from heaven... But the wisdom
that comes from heaven is first of all pure; then peace-loving,
considerate, submissive, full of mercy and good fruit, impartial
and sincere. (James 3:13-17)*

I think humility is a difficult quality to gain. A friend used to call me "Sister Sorry." I am one of those people who always thinks I'm at fault. I easily feel guilty. I apologize a lot. Also, I hate being the center of attention and will offer that to anyone else, but not because I'm humble; I'm just an introvert. I am fully aware that my personality is not humble. I am easily embarrassed. No one thinks of that as humble! Humility is a whole other entity. It does not consist of thinking negatively about oneself; it is thinking of others first. A humble person finally gets around to thinking about themselves and they think lovingly of self (Mark 12:31), but they are not obsessed with thoughts of self, either negative or positive. God likes humble people!

He has scattered those who are proud in their inmost thoughts...but has lifted up the humble. (Luke 1:51-52)

God opposes the proud but gives grace to the humble. (Philippians 2:6)

Humility sets apart the church of God. It puts his wisdom on display. It demonstrates an extremely appealing characteristic of God. It draws people to him even though it is not what they typically think of when they think of the nature of God. Happy day! We get to surprise them! It showcases our relationships as being founded in love and wisdom. Jesus said that his disciples would be known by their love (John 13:35). It is almost always appealing to people to see disciples able to "put up with one another" in love (Colossians 3:13 NIRV). It's why Paul told the Ephesian church, "Be completely humble and gentle; be patient, bearing with one another in love" (Ephesians 4:2).

So we are called to *complete* humility! I have seen that now and then. It's beautiful and it compels a respect in me that no knowledge or eloquence ever has. I think most people are affected that way.

It must be why Peter said, "Finally, all of you, be like-minded, be sympathetic, love one another, be compassionate and humble" (I Peter 3:8). Being agreeable, thoughtful, loving—this is the atmosphere Jesus wants us to live in within his church. It offers a security and a sense of belonging that could never come from a group characterized by everyone looking out for themselves. Like a magnet, humility attracts; but pride repels. We have a humble God and a humble Savior. Humility is not listed in Galatians 5, but it is definitely a fruit of God's Spirit.

• Meditation •

You save the humble but bring low those whose eyes are haughty.

— Psalm 116:5

We must want for others, not for ourselves alone.
—Eleanor Roosevelt

Chapter 14

Holy Submission

It may surprise you to find me including submission as an aspect of God's character. To whom would God submit? The thought is ludicrous if we think that only the underling submits to the superior. Since there is no one superior to God, how can God be submissive? Yet in our arrogance we think God should submit to (comply with) whatever we think is best. Our prayers are an issue of relationship and trust; our requests are not orders! Yet sometimes, I fear, we feel that God should do it our way on our time schedule, and we can get bitter if he doesn't. God has a submissive spirit to even hear us, much less to comply with our requests.

God will change circumstances and change his plans yielding to the requests of man. He is approachable and flexible. He can subdue his own inclinations even though they are always righteous.

There are many examples of God's submission in the Bible. He was willing to alter his plans to destroy Sodom and Gomorrah at the request of Abraham (Genesis 18:16–33). He abandoned his plan to send a destructive plague to rebellious, ungrateful Israel and submitted to Moses' plea to spare them (Numbers14:11–20).

When Hezekiah begged for more years of life, God defied nature and granted him fifteen more years on earth (II Kings 20:1–11).

Jesus submitted to ungodly, oppressive authorities and called us to do the same when he said, "Give back to Caesar what is Caesar's and to God what is God's" (Mark 12:13–17). He submitted to his mother against the timeline God had set when he turned water into wine (John 2:1–12). He submitted to his Father in Gethsemane by moving forward with the plan of bearing our sins on the cross (Matthew 26:36–27:66). In the flesh Jesus took on the same submissive position toward God to which we are called. God submitted to our need for salvation at unimaginable personal cost. He will always submit to our needs. He will sometimes submit to our wants, but if our needs and our wants are in conflict, it is our needs that will always win his heart and action.

Sometimes we say, "Not as I will, but as you will," in imitation of Jesus (Matthew 26:39), but often it's a cushion against our disappointment in case he doesn't submit to our wishes. Jesus said it in complete humble dependence and trust. Jesus also submitted to our needs by dying in our place.

Submission is not a popular concept in Western culture, where independence and equality are supremely valued. We don't like the idea of "giving in" to someone else. We accept it in the workplace where roles dictate hierarchy, but even then submission is often begrudged.

In my family there's a myth (I guess it's a myth) passed down through generations that a Texas ancestor insisted on being buried standing up, facing west, his rifle and whiskey jug at his side. It is said that he ordered this posture saying, "I bowed to no one in life and I'll bow to no one in death." What a heritage of pride I have—yikes! This man for sure hated submission.

The Greek word for submit is *hupotasso*. It means to humble self, to yield, to set in array under. A submissive person is deferential, compliant, cooperative. Contrary to the Victorian perspective, submission is a gender-neutral virtue. It is not just about wives submitting to husbands. And it is not just about external obedience; it's about a heart attitude that may result in compliance.

Submission should never result in a compromise of godly conviction. But remember, even when we have to say "no" to a request or demand, we are submitting to the *need* of the person who is making the request. When Shadrach, Meshach, and Abednego refused to bow down to Nebuchadnezzar's gold image, it was exactly what Nebuchadnezzar needed—an example of godly courage. It resulted in Nebuchadnezzar becoming a believer and changing the laws of Babylon and the future of the Israelite nation (Daniel 3:1–30).

A refusal to submit to authorities may not always have such dramatically positive results. Think of the God-submissive disciples in the book of Acts. Many became martyrs because of their submission to God instead of men.

One faithful woman, Cathy, defied her husband's insistence that she not attend church. She was submitting to God and to her husband's need to witness a true disciple's devotion to the body of Christ. She was humble, sweetly fulfilling every role as his wife, but she always put Jesus first. It took twelve years of setting an example of a love for God and his church before her husband finally became a disciple too. Certainly, not every story will end as happily as Cathy's, but submission will be rewarded by God, whether the earthly prize is evident or not.

Submission may be the character trait to which we are called that exhibits the most strength. Any weakling can be stubborn and intractable. Humility is no easily adopted trait, and submission is impossible without the foundation of humility. Some are resistant to submission based on the fear that it will make them a doormat or a weakling. In truth, submission displays power—the power to have control over our will, to relinquish our rights, and to be cooperative and yield to another, however unworthy they may be. Submission is strong and courageous and beautiful. It is holy.

• Meditation •

Submit yourselves for the Lord's sake to every human authority.

— I Peter 2:13

We need grace in order to be able to live in such a way as to qualify
ourselves to receive grace. —Aldous Huxley

Chapter 15

Holy Mercy Holy Grace

God extends mercy as an outpouring of his love. Mercy, then, gives birth to grace. Indeed, love, mercy, and grace are inseparable. The greatest gift of God's grace is salvation, but that is the ultimate gift, not the only gift. Someone once defined grace this way: "blessings bestowed when wrath was owed."

But because of his great love for us, God, who is rich in mercy, made us alive with Christ even while we were dead in our transgressions–it is by grace you have been saved. (Ephesians 2:4-5, emphasis added)

God's merciful love is so magnanimous that it reaches out to every human being. He purposely placed each of us, believer or nonbeliever, in the exact position in our lives where we would be most likely to recognize our need for him and respond to his grace (Acts 17:24–27). And it is not just a little bit of grace he gives us; it is grace that he "lavished on us" (Ephesians 1:7–8).

Mercy is a beautiful quality. At one time or another we all have longed for mercy. In a couple of places in the KJV, the Greek word *eleos* is not just translated mercy, but "tender mercy" (Luke 1:78; James 5:11). This Greek word means kindness, beneficence, compassion, and forbearance toward the unworthy or little deserving. It includes the idea of pity; we don't like to be pitied, but how desperately we need the tenderness of a God who can pity us in our fallen human state! This capacity of God for loving pity and tender mercy finds him with open arms to warmly embrace us and offer us grace.

In II Corinthians 1:3 Paul called God "the Father of compassion" (NIV), or "the Father of mercies" (KJV). Paul spoke of grace in every letter he wrote—eighty times in thirteen books. In Paul's letter to Titus, he summed up the relationship between mercy and grace and the miraculous result:

> But when the kindness and love of God our Savior appeared, he saved us, not because of righteous things we had done, but because of his mercy. He saved us through the washing of rebirth and renewal by the Holy Spirit, whom he poured out on us generously through Jesus Christ our Savior, so that, having been justified by his grace, we might become heirs having the hope of eternal life. (Titus 3:4-7)

God has every right to expect us to be deeply affected by his mercy and grace. Paul told the Roman churches that as they considered God's mercy, it should motivate them to offer their entire selves to him as a "living sacrifice" (Romans 12:1). He told Titus that it is the grace of God, not the commandments of God, that teaches us to say "No" to sin (Titus 2:11–12). We cannot approach mercy intellectually if we are to be moved in this way. It must feel personal and awe-inspiring and fill us with gratitude.

I admit this is hard for me to grasp. I understand the mercy part better than I do the grace part—grace, that free, unmerited gift. It doesn't add up. It is not that I haven't witnessed it or been a recipient even in an earthly form from benefactors who owed me nothing. It is just that there is some sort of balance sheet in my head, and the ruler of the universe who has a perfect standard is too far above me and I am too sinful. It is not like I am in some space of moral neutrality and am, therefore, graciously left in limbo; it is that I am sinful in every area of offense toward God and what I justly deserve is damnation.

I can't explain grace. I have read some spiritual books about it by brilliant spiritual thinkers, and I recommend a study of grace. Maybe you will have more insight than I. While I'm reading these books, they make a ton of sense and offer wonderful hope and comfort, although even then, they can make me feel guilty for not living in a constant state of exultant bliss over the grace extended to me. But as soon as I close the book and the words on the page are not in front of me, it seems illogical again. Maybe that's the point. Grace is illogical. Maybe this free gift of salvation can only be explained in light of a love and mercy beyond our comprehension (Ephesians 3:16–19). Grace must be accepted as a gift and understood by faith. Additionally, we are warned against trying to earn grace (Galatians 5:4). That makes sense, because it would be the height of arrogance to assume that we could do something to deserve God's extraordinary grace.

Grace, in reference to salvation, is repeatedly called a gift in the book of Romans (5:15–17). However, salvation is not the only gift of God's grace. Any blessing we receive is a gift of his grace. We often think we have earned the blessings in our lives, but we should abandon that thinking immediately, for "from the fullness of his grace, we have all received one blessing after another" (John 1:16 NIV1984). God doesn't grudgingly show mercy; he delights to show mercy (Micah 7:18).

As with the other traits of God's nature, we are called to imitate him. In this case, we are called to be merciful and gracious. That calling in itself is a gift of grace. Grace must be demonstrated; it is not just an idea or a feeling or a kind inclination toward someone. God believes in us. He is willing to call us his own, and he delights in us when we resemble him. He uses this imitation of his nature to impact a lost world and bless our fellowship in his church.

Showing mercy is not always easy. As with the other gifts given by the Holy Spirit, we should earnestly pray for his assistance in growing in these gifts and graces. It is challenging to be merciful toward the people most in need of mercy. God asks for more than just meeting practical needs. He has specifically gifted some of us to be merciful. The call is to show mercy cheerfully (Romans 12:8). This is not always an easy attitude to maintain, but it is what is most needed because mercy offered grudgingly doesn't supply the same holy comfort (to the giver or the receiver). Sometimes we can be critical and judgmental and feel very justified, but the Bible tells us that "judgment without mercy will be shown to anyone who has not been merciful" (James 2:13).

God calls us to shine in a dark world. We may have to go against our natures until mercy, compassion, grace, and forgiveness are our default responses to the world around us. Being like the world will never set us apart. And that's what holiness is all about—being set apart.

• Meditation •

Grateful for his mercy and grace:

...always giving thanks to God the Father for everything, in the name of our Lord Jesus Christ.

— Ephesians 5:10

The highest wisdom consists in distinguishing between good and evil.
—Socrates (470–399BC)

Chapter 16

Holy Wisdom

I think Socrates almost got it right. I think the highest wisdom is not just in distinguishing good from evil, but in internalizing the good by obeying God.

God embodies wisdom. His thoughts are wise; his actions are wise; his instructions to us are extremely wise. Every caution he offers us is wise. Fools may think God's requirements are unnecessarily restrictive, but they are wrong.

There are not enough superlatives to describe the wisdom of God. A clear spiritual perspective will allow us to see the vastness of creation as only a miniscule example of God's wisdom. As Friedrich von Schiller (1759–1805) said, "The universe is one of God's thoughts. And if we grow to have faith and search out those thoughts, we can become wise." We are not born wise. What we are born with is the need to acknowledge, delight in, and honor the wisdom of God. Angels and elders and other heavenly beings fall on their faces before his throne:

Amen!
Praise and glory
and wisdom and thanks and honor
and power and strength
be to our God for ever and ever.
Amen! (Revelation 7:12)

Wisdom is learned in increments, and God is its only source. Some wisdom is learned through study. Some is learned through seeking the advice of others (Proverbs 13:10). Some is gained through experience and trial and error (Hebrews 5:14), like don't touch the stove—it's hot! While God offers wisdom freely, it is often hard won and never automatic.

Even fools have some wisdom, but whatever wisdom they have is a gift of God. We are all born with some helpful instincts that enable us to learn some truths quickly, but being educated or articulate or clever or having a high IQ does not equal wisdom. Maybe the most familiar example of this is Nietzsche. He was smart and knowledgeable but not wise. His brilliant observations are studied in every university philosophy class. But he famously said, "God is dead." As an atheist, he didn't mean that there was a God who had literally died, but that as an "enlightened" society, we no longer needed to invent the concept of God. His arrogance eclipsed his wisdom when he also said, "There cannot be a God because if there were I could not believe that I am not he." Nietzsche is dead now, so he has been disabused of those misconceptions.

When pride comes, then comes disgrace,
    but with humility comes wisdom. (Proverbs 11:2)

*Woe to those who are wise in their own eyes
and clever in their own sight. (Isaiah 5:21)*

The original Greek and Hebrew words for wisdom could be translated as sagacity or the careful use of knowledge. Synonyms may include sensible, judicious, reasonable, and circumspect. Heavenly wisdom has companions: "I, wisdom, dwell together with prudence. I possess knowledge and discretion" (Proverbs 8:12). Wisdom hangs out with prudence, knowledge, and discretion—impressive companions!

King David defined wisdom as "the fear of the Lord" (Psalm 111:10). And his son Solomon (to whom God gifted more wisdom than any other human ever possessed [I Kings 4:29]) echoed that exact thought in Proverbs 9:10. The fear of the Lord is confusing for some. Abraham Joshua Herschel (1907–1972) accurately paraphrased these scriptures, "The awe of God is wisdom." I like to describe wisdom as trusting that God means what he says. Herschel also said, "Wisdom is the ability to look at all things from the point of view of God."

We are blessed to have an infallible source for that viewpoint—the Bible. We can only look at things from God's point of view by knowing what his viewpoint is. That requires being students of his word, where he reveals his mind and heart, as well as his will for us.

The value of holy wisdom is incalculable. Proverbs 8:11 states that "wisdom is far more precious than rubies, and nothing you desire can compare with her." Proverbs 16:16 says, "How much better it is to get wisdom than gold, to get insight rather than silver!" Impressive, considering the human tendency to covet silver and gold. Most of us are somewhat dull to wisdom's comparative worth. Even analogies—when we are aware of them—often fail to have the appropriate impact. Consider this one in Proverbs 24:3–4:

> *By wisdom a house is built,*
>   *and through understanding it is established;*
> *through knowledge its rooms are filled*
>   *with rare and beautiful treasures.*

God has certainly tried within his word to help us understand!

My granddaughter Emma graduated from college in 2020 with a double major in accounting and economics. God offers a PhD in wisdom that is all about the economics of righteousness. Proverbs 23:23 says, "Buy truth and do not sell it—wisdom, instruction and insight as well." The impassioned plea to all of us in Proverbs 4:5–7 reveals God's longing for us to find this treasure:

> *Get wisdom, get understanding;*
>   *do not forget my words or turn away from them.*
> *Do not forsake wisdom, and she will protect you;*
>   *love her, and she will watch over you.*
> *The beginning of wisdom is this: Get wisdom.*
>   *Though it cost all you have, get understanding.*

It is probably unwise for me to mention it (but I can't help it and I don't assign any intent of God to it), but I love that wisdom gets the feminine pronoun here. I say that in all humility (maybe).

Solomon complained in Proverbs 17:16 that fools have the same access to wisdom as the pure in heart. The difference is that God's wisdom will be desirable to the pure hearted, but not to those seeking self-satisfaction (Matthew 13:18-23; II Timothy 4:3). In Colossians 2:20ff, the Apostle Paul warns against accepting things that "have the appearance of wisdom." We must be alert and astute about what we accept as wisdom, because there are two kinds (James 3:13–17).

Humility...comes from wisdom. (James 3:13)

I think it is almost comical (but actually sad) that so much of what is considered wise on earth is heralded by arrogant pundits. Arrogance is the polar opposite of humility. They seem to think that volume and vocabulary prove their point. Oh, shame!

But the wisdom that comes from heaven is first of all pure; then peace-loving, considerate, submissive, full of mercy and good fruit, impartial and sincere. (James 3:17)

This is not the description many people would offer as the trademark essentials of wisdom, but I love this! It is comforting to be assured that the wisdom that has real value may not be lauded by the world. I can stand tall in the wisdom that God offers, without apology or feeling inferior in any way. It is not that I have arrived; I am farther away from wise than I expected to be by this age, but at least God has given me a clear picture. I believe in God's wisdom and I know where to find it. I reject the wisdom of the world, although it can be tempting, and I admit I fail sometimes.

For the wisdom of the world is foolishness in God's sight. As it is written:... "The Lord knows that the thoughts of the wise are futile." (I Corinthians 3:19-20)

The wise will be put to shame;...
Since they have rejected the word of the LORD,

what kind of wisdom do they have? (Jeremiah 8:9)

I rest my hope in the truth that Christ "has become for us wisdom from God—that is, our righteousness, holiness and redemption" (I Corinthians 1:30). I love knowing that if I am wise enough to know I lack wisdom, it's just a prayer away and God will not think less of me for my neediness (James 1:5). And I also delight in knowing that "the foolishness of God is wiser than human wisdom" (I Corinthians 1:25). Thank you, God! Wisdom is a treasure and ours for the asking.

• Meditation •

Oh, the depth of the riches of the wisdom and the knowledge of God! How unsearchable his judgments, and his paths beyond tracing out! "Who has known the mind of the Lord? Or who has been his counselor?" "Who has ever given to God, that God should repay them?" For from him and through him and for him are all things.
To him be the glory forever! Amen.

— Romans 11:33-36

Truth is so obscured nowadays and lies so well established that
unless we love the truth we shall never recognize it.
—Blaise Pascal

Chapter 17

Holy Truth

I wonder whether anyone over the age of five has never told a lie. I am pretty sure that my first lie was an effort to stay out of trouble: "Nope! I didn't do it!" I wish my lying had stopped there. The problem with lying is not just that we may be found out on earth; the real problem is that it can send us to hell. "But the cowardly, the unbelieving, the vile, the murderers, the sexually immoral, those who practice magic arts, the idolaters, and all liars—they will be consigned to the fiery lake of burning sulfur. This is the second death" (Revelations 21:8). Lying seems like such a trivial offense compared to the other sins on this list. It's not.

It's embarrassing to confess a lie. I guess any sin is embarrassing to confess, but some seem harder than others. I think most of the lies I have told were over petty things when the truth would have served much better. "I'd like to go anywhere you'd like to go"; "That dress looks just fine on you"; "No, I'm not upset." The truth will *always* serve better if we want to please God.

It's scary to know that we are aligning ourselves with Satan when we lie. He is "a liar and the father of lies" (John 8:44). Mainly he lies to us! In the war for our souls he seeks to deceive us every day. Sometimes he convinces us that lies are justified, even kind. You know, the ones we call "little white lies."

Once after I'd had surgery, friends were bringing us meals. Their generosity had me freezing the oversupply. One friend inquired a week or so later whether I liked her casserole. "Delicious!" I replied. I was embarrassed when I had to go back and explain that, because I didn't want her to feel I was ungrateful, I complimented her cooking even though I had not yet tasted her culinary gift. She was gracious, but I could tell she was disappointed. It would have been much easier if I had just said, "You know what? We received more than we could eat right away, but I'm happy to have a backup supply. Thank you so much! I'll let you know how we enjoyed it as soon as it's thawed and devoured."

Truth is refreshing! God wants us to love the truth. It is refreshing to tell the truth. It is also refreshing to know we are being told the truth (even when we would rather not hear it). I feel secure around people I can trust to tell me the truth, and I even like them better for it. That includes the people who have been brave enough and honest enough to return and confess that they told me a lie.

The fruit of the light consists in all goodness, righteousness and truth. (Ephesians 5:9)

My first job, outside of being a stay-at-home mom, had me seeking advice from a friend who was a long-time professional. She said, "Always tell the truth. If you make a mistake, own it right away. It will set you apart from the finger-pointers and make you respected." It was great advice. I was often in positions in which it would have been tempting to lie or just remain silent and hope no one noticed or cared that I had goofed. My boss asked me to lie three times in one day when I first went to work at his company. He was so comfortable with "the check is in the mail," that he didn't even realize he was asking me to lie. I remember thinking I would get fired when I told him, "I won't lie for you. But it will work out great because I won't lie *to* you either." I didn't get fired.

I love that "it is impossible for God to lie" (Hebrews 6:18). I can trust everything about him and every word he speaks. Jesus, too, claimed truth as his very being when he said, "I am the way and the truth and the life" (John 14:6). Truth—that's who he is. What does the Spirit of God consist of? Truth! Joy! Peace! And every other fruit of the Spirit and most likely some awesome stuff we don't even have the vocabulary to express or the capacity to grasp, but it is all perfect and pure. These "et cetera ingredients" of God's Spirit are beyond our understanding and our imaginations—wonder of wonders!

Truth—when Jesus appeared before Pilate (who had the civil power to spare him the cross) Jesus told him boldly, "The reason I was born and came into the world is to testify to the truth. Everyone on the side of truth listens to me" (John 18:37). Pilate replied with a rhetorical question: "What is truth?" He probably thought his question was clever. He just turned and walked away without waiting for Jesus to answer. He didn't stick around to listen.

There's a great lesson in this account. We need to persevere and hear Jesus' answer to this question. Absolute truth really does exist, and we have access to it, but it will take some attention and focus and maybe some time. This truth offers us divine knowledge and godliness and can save us eternally (Titus 1:1–2; Ephesians 1:13). This holy truth has the ability to guide our growth to become more like Jesus. That's called sanctification. It is how we can increasingly put on the attributes of God and fulfill the prayer Jesus prayed for us (John 17:17). Sanctification means being set apart for a holy purpose.

We can hold this truth in our hands (the Bible); we *must* it hold in our hearts. The world is full of lies—even the religious world. We should study the Scriptures diligently to confirm truth for ourselves. It is an adventure to search out the heart of God and find the jewels of truth. There is no end to this treasure. Our lives will end before we have discovered all the wonders of truth in his word, but our lives will be increasingly enriched by the effort.

> Never take your word of truth from my mouth,
>   for I have put my hope in your laws. (Psalm 119:43)

• Meticulation •

For the word of the Lord is right and true;
he is faithful in all he does.

— Psalm 33:4

A man is most accurately judged by how he treats those who are
not in a position either to retaliate or to reciprocate.
—Paul Eldridge (1888–1982)

Chapter 18

Holy Jealousy, Holy Justice

I have coupled these two topics because they have something
in common. We have been talking about attributes of God that we
can and should unreservedly imitate, but jealousy and justice are
different. They are part of the nature of God but restricted in their
application to us. They must be handled judiciously (always) and
avoided by Christians (usually). The fruits of the Spirit have no
boundaries or restrictions for Christians; jealousy and justice do.
God, in his perfection, is the only one able to embody them with
righteous discernment. God is a jealous God, and he is a just God
(Exodus 20:5; Deuteronomy 32:4).

Holy Jealousy

Most often jealousy here on earth is a negative thing. Its expressions can range from bitterness to murder. It is one of the easier sins to justify or deny, even to ourselves, and that alone makes
it dangerous. It destroys friendships, marriages, and the hearts of

those who allow it to live within them. This is why jealousy is repeatedly called out as sin in the Bible (Romans 13:13; I Corinthians 3:3; II Corinthians 12:20; Galatians 5:19–20).

God has the only perfect claim to jealousy. Perhaps marriage vows give us a right to be jealous if our mate is unfaithful, but it's a thorny proposition. Even in marriage we are hobbled in our ability to maintain godly boundaries on this volatile emotion. We can leave this to God. I believe that with perfect discernment God longs for repentance, not retribution. It is both reassuring and sobering to know that God will be jealous on our behalf. When vows are broken, it is not only a spouse who has been sinned against, but God as well.

Uniquely, God is capable of pure altruistic jealousy. God's jealousy is not about a bruised ego. His Spirit hurts when we hurt ourselves. He calls us to his nature because he wants us to love righteousness. We should try to learn altruistic jealousy. The Apostle Paul had it down: "I am jealous for you with a godly jealousy" (II Corinthians 11:2).

Holy Justice

The justice of God is all about scrupulous fairness. Paul told the church in Thessalonica simply, "God is just" (II Thessalonians 1:6). There is no fuzziness where God's fairness is concerned. He is perfectly just, and we would do well never to pass judgment on his fairness (II Chronicles 12:6; Nehemiah 9:13; Job 34:12).

God wants us to be just. He loves justice (Psalm 11:7). That means we must be conscientious about what is fair and make sure we keep rigid boundaries on our own righteousness in our dealings with others.

He has shown you, O mortal, what is good.
  And what does the LORD require of you?
To act justly and to love mercy
  and to walk humbly with your God. (Micah 6:8)

God makes it clear that we are in charge of justice only as it applies to our own behavior; we are not to judge others. Our unfortunate tendency is to judge others by our opinions and prejudices. Researchers have found that we cut ourselves slack that we don't cut others when we judge. We tend to judge others by their behavior and ourselves by our intent. Of course, we always think our intentions were good! It is understandable that God asks us to leave the definition of justice and the judgment of others to him. We would be wise not to use imitating God as an excuse to be jealous or judgmental. There are many things best left to God. These two might top the list!

• Meditation •

Jesus: "By myself I can do nothing; I judge only as I hear, and my judgment is just, for I seek not to please myself but him who sent me."

— John 5:30

The main object of religion is not to get a man into heaven,
but to get heaven into him. —Thomas Hardy

Chapter 19
Holy Knowledge

Fruits that combine to reveal who God is are highlighted in the Bible (Galatians 5:22–23). The previous chapters and meditation prompts in this book have been focused on those beautiful, desirable characteristics. As Christians, we are meant to grow spiritually, making those fruits a part of our own natures. The wonderful result is that we look more and more like him and know him in a most intimate way.

Contrary to the isolation sometimes associated with holy people (for example, taking vows of silence and solitude), holy knowledge does not set us apart from others as much as it sets us apart from ourselves. The Bible calls us to put off our old natures and put on the new. With tender hearts, we will seek to put off our flawed natures in favor of his. It is what makes us holy, set apart in an unholy world (Colossians 3:8–10).

I have found aiming for holiness to be a challenging venture. I fell in love with God a bit before I understood the imperative of growing to be like him. It was hard for me to concentrate on what he was calling me to become because I was consumed with the new understanding of my sins. This played into my nature to be easily overcome by guilt. Guilt should call us to repentance, not self-hatred. It comes easier to me to focus on regret than to focus on the goal of holiness. I admired God enormously, but it had not yet occurred to me to try to imitate the fruits of his Spirit. Writing this book has been deeply convicting. I have been made increasingly aware of how far I need to grow toward God's call to be holy.

Knowing God is not just about information or acquaintance; it starts there, but it is much more—it is a knowledge that must be embodied. Lots of people know about God and many are acquainted with him, but few know him in the biblical sense. Holy knowledge is as intimate as being one flesh in marriage (Ephesians 5:31–32).

Knowing God is not about perfection—only Jesus accomplished that down here—but it is about maturing into the attributes of his character. We'll get there someday (I John 3:2; I Corinthians 13:12). On earth, as we grow to be more and more like God, we become the answer to Jesus' prayer in John 17:21, "that all of them may be one, Father, just as you are in me and I am in you. May they also be one so that the world may believe that you have sent me." Jesus wants us to be in him and the Father in the way that they are in each other. Mind-blowing! Jesus wants a unity with us that is so deep that the world will be able to "see" God through our lives. We displace our own flawed natures with his—one thought, one act, one day at a time.

> Ask God who made you to keep on remaking you.
> –Norman Vincent Peale

To know God, we can't just coast through life calling ourselves

Christians without a daily effort to be like him. There must be progress and growth both in our hearts and in our behavior. We'll have victories and failures, but we must strive to be set apart. As we seek to claim the fruits of his Spirit in our own natures, we must pray for God's power to find peace that remains even in the midst of turmoil; patience that wins out over fretful agitation; kindness that extends even to the unkind; goodness that is visible in our actions; a growing faithfulness to the values God has taught us; self-control that triumphs over selfishness and indulgence—and love over all. It is not simply that God *has* these attributes; he *is* these attributes! The Christian life is an adventure in knowing the heart of God and becoming men and women after his own heart and behavior.

When we become Christians, we experience eternal life. In John 17:3, we are told, "Now this is eternal life: that they know you, the only true God, and Jesus Christ, whom you have sent." We are not waiting for eternal life to begin when we die or when Jesus comes back, we are living eternal life now by knowing God in every sense of that word.

God wants a very intimate connection with us. Paul understood this. It is why it was a constant request of his for other disciples. He told the Christians in Ephesus, "I keep asking that...God... may give you the Spirit of wisdom and revelation, so that you may know him better" (Ephesians 1:17). Similarly, Paul "continually" asked God to fill the Colossian disciples with "all the wisdom and understanding that the Spirit gives," so that they might "live a life worthy of the Lord and please him in every way: bearing fruit in every good work, growing in the knowledge of God" (Colossians 1:9–10). We should pray for each other to grow in this special kind of knowledge.

"He defended the cause of the poor and needy,
  and so all went well.
Is that not what it means to know me?"
  declares the LORD. (Jeremiah 22:16)

Having been made in the image of God, we have a full capacity through his Spirit to mature toward all that he is. As we are in the process of this growth, we take on his appearance. We will never know him fully until we see him face to face. But it is the pursuit of this inner knowledge that is the aim of the Christian life: to know him with our hearts—our emotions and motivations (John 15:12); and our souls—the essence of who we are, including our personalities (John 17:25–26); and our minds—at least all that our intellects can absorb (II Timothy 3:16); and our strength through our service to others (James 2:14–17). It is one of the reasons he gave us his Spirit: "so that you may know him better" (Ephesians 1:17). Our purpose here on earth is to live out the nature of God.

It is dangerous to think that biblical scholarship alone offers the kind of knowledge that God wants us to have. Consider what Paul said: "Those who think they know something do not yet know as they ought to know. But whoever loves God is known by God" (I Corinthians 8:2–3).

Love—the beginning and source of every fruit of the Spirit. For many years I have used these fruits as the standard by which I measure myself. When I have the presence of mind to stop and check myself, these fruits always correct my course. I have learned that when I get busy "doing good" I can become impatient, short-tempered, anxious, and unkind to those around me. Farewell to the "good" in "doing good"! To know God is not just to accomplish some good stuff. Woe is me!

Believing that God is beside us and within us not only gives us hope that we can change and the confidence to try; it gives us the very real and practical inner working of his Spirit to transform us (II Corinthians 1:21–22, 3:18). God's Spirit will always nudge us toward pure attitudes of the heart and righteous behavior. It is how we are transformed into the likeness of God. It's good to occasionally ask ourselves, "How's my transformation going?"

> *Examine yourselves to see if your faith is genuine. Test yourselves. Surely you know that Jesus Christ is among you; if not, you have failed the test of genuine faith. (II Corinthians 13:5 NLT)*

Our goal is to know God and to be known by him. It is the intimacy of his Spirit within us. The caution is that busyness and good deeds will not get us into heaven. Jesus warned that judgment day would find some folks surprised when God says, "I never knew you. Away from me!" (Matthew 7:22–23). Why would an all-knowing God say to anyone that he never knew them? I think it's that his Spirit doesn't recognize the spirit of those who are not seeking to embody his nature. Being religious and busy and clinging to certain doctrines does not equal having the heart of God or the character of God. He wants a heart connection with us that will last through all eternity when all the "doing" is past and earth has slipped away.

Jesus once told a group of religious leaders, "I know you. I know you do not have the love of God in your hearts" (John 5:42). And Paul told the Corinthian church, "Whoever loves God is known by God" (I Corinthians 8:3). Love by God's standards means obedience (I John 2:3). Obedience to God certainly includes some doing, but it must come from a heart connected to God by being in the process of transformation into his likeness.

121

I know, my God, that you test the heart and are pleased with integrity. (I Chronicles 29:17)

It is harder to examine our hearts than it is to take note of our accomplishments. It is also way too easy to think we have a love that impresses God when we are impressed with our own sentimentality. Sentimental people can feel emotionally moved by the cross (and we certainly all should be) and delighted by the Scriptures (and that's a good thing too) without having the kind of active love God is looking for. A quiet sentimentality may never motivate a pursuit of God's nature that actively lives out his love.

And just a busy life is not what he is hoping to see in us either. It is the inner transformation prompting unselfish actions that aligns our spirits with his. Everything about God's love is unselfish.

All the prayers we offer for God's help in this pursuit and the efforts we exert should be focused on knowing him—not as an acquaintance, but as a part of our very being. It is our God-given destiny to be infused and saturated with his character. It is the very reason he made us in his image. On earth, only Jesus bore the exact image of his Father, but day by day we can grow closer and closer to that image. When I meet him on the last day I want him to recognize me as his child because my spirit has grown to look like his. I want to have an unmistakable family resemblance!

• Meditation •

You, God, are my God, earnestly I seek you; I thirst for you, my whole being longs for you, in a dry and parched land where there is no water.

— Psalm 63:1

Hand in Hand with God:

Finding
Your Path to
FORGIVENESS

Linda Brumley

Books by Linda Brumley
at www.ipibooks.com

GOLDEN RULE

What God
Expects of
Every
Disciple

MEMBERSHIP

John Oakes with Ron and Linda Brumley

Books by Linda Brumley
at www.ipibooks.com

Gordon Ferguson

God, are We Good?

Can I Know for Sure?

PRINCIPLES
OF LOVING
ONE-ANOTHER
RELATIONSHIPS

Discipling
REDEFINED

Editor
CHRIS CARTER

Books available from www.ipibooks.com

Books available from www.ipibooks.com

www.ipibooks.com